To mi_____ !

the _____ ?

God be upon you always.

Dr. _____ (signature)

5-2-11

MW00940154

A Gentle Tug

Howard Dailey and Barbara Pannell

WESTBOW
P R E S S
A DIVISION OF THOMAS NELSON

Copyright © 2011 Howard Dailey and Barbara Pannell

All rights reserved. No part of this book may be used or reproduced by any means, graphic, electronic, or mechanical, including photocopying, recording, taping or by any information storage retrieval system without the written permission of the publisher except in the case of brief quotations embodied in critical articles and reviews.

WestBow Press books may be ordered through booksellers or by contacting:

WestBow Press
A Division of Thomas Nelson
1663 Liberty Drive
Bloomington, IN 47403
www.westbowpress.com
1-(866) 928-1240

Because of the dynamic nature of the Internet, any web addresses or links contained in this book may have changed since publication and may no longer be valid. The views expressed in this work are solely those of the author and do not necessarily reflect the views of the publisher, and the publisher hereby disclaims any responsibility for them.

Any people depicted in stock imagery provided by Thinkstock are models, and such images are being used for illustrative purposes only.

Certain stock imagery © Thinkstock.

ISBN: 978-1-4497-1335-5 (sc)
ISBN: 978-1-4497-1337-9 (dj)
ISBN: 978-1-4497-1336-2 (e)

Library of Congress Control Number: 2011923317

All Scripture quotations are taken from the King James Version of the Bible.

Printed in the United States of America

WestBow Press rev. date: 3/16/2011

To my parents
The late Newton and Ermine Dailey
Whose quiet and gentle spirits taught me about the love of God

Contents

Preface

Life being a journey, we seldom see the forks in the road, until they suddenly – and sometimes dramatically – appear before us. Although not on our agenda, they're never a surprise to God. Many times we feel that our lives have been unfairly interrupted. Even though in reality we sometimes fly by the seat of our pants, our plans for the future have been derailed and much to our frustration and dismay, often we cannot see the forest for the trees. God always has a better plan in place, even though at the time it certainly doesn't seem that way. Even as we look back at life and we *think* we understand, any suppositions on our part would only be a guess as to God's eternal plan.

The events in my life have been amazing even to me as I look back. God's call on my life, the accident, my death and recovery, ministering, pastoring a church and running a business fulltime left me with little time to write. Over the years I've realized the events of my life were meant to be shared with other people, and as I began using the events in my sermons, and as I worked in my business sharing these things with my customers, I began to realize that a book was part of God's plan. Over and over, people would ask me when I was going to write the book. The book would show how God uses ordinary people in extraordinary ways. How was I to accomplish this task? God was soon to put someone in my path that would – in due time – write the book.

In 1991, a customer came to me for a reflexology session. Upon remarkable improvement in her health, she soon brought her family and friends to me, and shortly after that I asked her to manage a store for me. Barbara Pannell, that once customer, has worked for me since that time. For years, as she worked, she listened to story after story of my life. She knew as well that a book needed to be written, and she even tried to help me find a writer. Then seemingly out-of-the-blue, as she was driving to work God interrupted her thoughts as she gazed into the eastern sunrise. *You are to write the book.* Without hesitation she said, "God, I'll hold the pencil. You tell me what to write." , believing that if He told her to write the book, he'd enable her to do it. Thus her journey began. That very day she took out pencil and paper to begin taking notes. *A Gentle Tug* was in progress. God always finishes what He begins. He never promises anything that He doesn't complete. This is the story of my life.

Introduction

The old hearse rumbled down the dusty country road, slowing down to take the curves. The driver knew there was no need to hurry; the accident victim had been dead for at least forty-five minutes. As the black wagon rounded the last bend, just before the site of the horrible motorcycle accident, the driver saw a crowd gathered at the roadside. There's always a crowd. Some stop to help, others just to gawk. All wonder what happened.

In the case of this accident, no one realized that what seemed to be a tragic ending would prove to be an astonishing beginning. A perfectly ordinary day was about to change—dramatically.

But First

In a tiny cabin in Tennessee, on a cold and snowy day in 1943, yet another child was born to Newton and Ermine Dailey. This was child thirteen out of fourteen. The seventh of seven sons made his entrance into this world. They named him Howard.

So many mouths to feed, yet never once did you hear them complain. Although there were many in this brood, never did they feel unwanted or unloved. Even though the family was crowded into one tiny cabin, there was always room for anyone in need.

The future seemed rather bleak, except for the fact that these children had loving parents with a mighty faith in God. Still, the saying about people who are "poor but don't know it" didn't apply to this bunch. The Daileys didn't have to be told! They were poor and they *knew* it, but they were a happy family and that is something not everybody can say.

Times were really hard growing up, clothes were usually hand me downs. The children all got new shoes once a year (in the fall, after the crops were sold). When they outgrew the shoes they would go barefoot for the remainder of the year. They never minded going without shoes in the summertime. The neighbors' children were in greater need, going barefoot even in the coldest of winter snows. Food was scarce, but the family willingly shared what they did have with others. The Daileys literally kept the neighbors from starving during some very difficult years.

The family wouldn't know the luxury of having electricity until the children were almost grown. They were a very close-knit family. With one of this size, close-knit was an understatement; to see just how many kids could sleep on one featherbed on cold nights – now *that* is what one calls close!

Just Surviving
(Howard's Story)

Being of Irish and Cherokee Indian descent, we came from very hardy stock. We were used to living in harsh environments, and we knew how to survive on the land and make do with what we had. We owned few material possessions, but we had an abundance of the things that mattered: love, respect for one another, and most importantly, faith in God.

Our Indian heritage played a great role in how we grew up. The signs of nature allowed us to discern the weather patterns, such as fast-approaching storms, and we learned how to prepare for an especially harsh winter. We observed everything, from the color of the wooly worms to the density of the hickory nutshells, from the thickness of the animals' fur to the unusual way leaves turned upside down when a storm was approaching. We didn't need television to predict the weather. To us, nature was much more reliable.

We knew how to garden and how to preserve the resulting vegetables for later use; how to raise chickens, hogs, and cattle for meat; and how to hunt wild game and fish to add to the family menu.

Mom gathered wild, aromatic herbs, just as she'd been taught by her folks. Some were used fresh, others dried for later use; some were for cooking, others for medicine. (God would one day place me in a unique business, selling herbs and nutritional supplements and using the age-old art of reflexology.)

We were sharecroppers, and eventually it came time for us to move from that snug little cabin to another farm with a little bigger home. We would manage a herd of cattle and a dairy on the new place, and of course there was the big garden to tend. It took a lot of hard work to put up enough food to get the family through those long, cold Tennessee winters.

This is the "bigger home" that the Dailey family moved into on the dairy farm.

We all had to help with the chores, but we still managed to find time to play. The girls played house, while the boys could usually be found shooting marbles, wrestling, or skinny-dipping in the nearest stream.

Many times, I enjoyed getting away by myself to ponder things. A towering sycamore tree grew in the lush, rolling meadow across the dusty road from our place. I was a little guy, and it was easy to grasp the bark with my bare feet and scamper to the very top. I'd settle down on a sturdy forked branch among the fluttering green leaves and feel the hot summer breeze brush against my warm skin. My secret place was at the very top of the tree. The sky always seemed bluer and the birds seemed to chirp louder up there. The song of the cicadas seemed to rise and fall to the rhythm of my breathing. I felt closer to God in that wonderful place, and I went there often. I'd think about the stories we learned in church, the very same ones Mom read to us from the old family Bible. Many times after supper, we'd gather around her feet, and she'd read as she rocked one of us.

One of my favorite Bible stories was about Zacchaeus, a short man who climbed a sycamore tree to see Jesus. I often wondered if *my* sycamore tree was the same one that Zacchaeus had climbed. Just *maybe* Jesus would walk by, see me up there, and ask if he could come by my house for supper.

I now know that those wonderings were a gentle tug from God on a little boy's heart.

I still enjoy the view from a treetop. As an adult, I often find myself in a tree stand in the dead of winter, pulling my collar up a little closer under my chin as the wind chills my face. I clutch the cold barrel of a rifle as I strain to hear the crackle of dry leaves that might indicate that the big buck that's been so elusive might finally be approaching. I hold my breath so as not to frighten him away, and I know that trees are *wonderful* thinking places—for little boys and big boys alike.

What a spunky bunch of ragtag kids we were. *Nobody* messed with the Dailey kids—there were just too many of us! Still, I was always a shy little guy. When somebody I didn't know came to our house, I often hid under the bed until they left. And yes, it got stuffy under there on a sultry summer day. There were always a couple of dust bunnies in tow when I finally slid out.

People from far and wide knew that our daddy, Newton Dailey, prayed out behind the barn. Daddy knew God wasn't hard of hearing, but he always said that praying loud never hurt anybody. If folks got within earshot, they knew all about our praises and our problems.

We attended the church closest to our house, either walking or riding in the wagon. When we rode in the wagon, it had to be prepared the night before by pushing it into the creek to submerge the wheels so that the wood would expand to fit the metal rims. As we made our way to church down the old dirt road, several other families would join us along the way. Wonderful hymns of praise and worship spontaneously rose to the heavens in beautiful layers of harmony as we walked or rode along. Even as a child, I realized something very special was taking place. The preacher didn't have to "prime the pump." The beginning of the service was just a continuation of what we had already been experiencing all along the road on our way to the service. One never forgets those special moments.

Once we arrived at church, our bunch filled up one entire pew. We were expected to behave, but boys will be boys. When we misbehaved, Mom pointed her stubby little finger at us. Once was allowed, but if that finger pointed a second time, we knew we were in *big* trouble when we got home. On those Sundays, I always ran to get in bed the minute we got home, so I could pretend to be asleep. While pretending, I prayed Mom had forgotten about my behavior. More often than not, though, just when I thought maybe she *had* forgotten this time, down came the covers, the britches, and all, and yee-ouch! I wouldn't be naughty in church again anytime soon!

The preacher often joined our family for a Sunday dinner. The visiting minister rode his mule to our house this particular day after church service. Many times just before he left to travel back to his home, our family would give him a gift of food to take with him. Sometimes it would be a chicken or perhaps some vegetables, however on this day Dad had something else in mind, something really special. After we had eaten dinner, Dad went to the smokehouse and took down a ham. He took out his hand-saw and cut it in two pieces. The preacher beamed! "Why, Newton, that's the nicest thing a man ever done for me!" I guess he must have been in a big hurry since he sure was fast in stuffing half a ham in each side of his saddlebags. "To think of sawing the ham in two pieces, just so it'd be easy for me to carry home!" Dad was dumbfounded at that statement but he didn't say a word, just adjusted the old cap and looked off in the distance. He didn't have the heart to tell the preacher that was the last piece of meat the family had. His good-natured intention was to give one half to him and to keep the other half for our hungry family. Dad was always generous to a fault but he didn't worry about it since he knew that God was always faithful to his word: *"Therefore I say unto you, take no thought for your life, what ye shall eat, or what you shall drink, nor yet for your body, what ye shall put on. Is not the life more than meat, and the body than raiment?"* (Matthew 6:25)

The Call

For weeks before what I refer to as "the call," God had been dealing with my heart. I was excited just being in church, knowing in my spirit that something wonderful was about to take place. God always seemed very near when I was sitting alone amid the branches of the sycamore tree. He felt close when my mom and dad and the other church members prayed for me too. Somehow, I knew that God was using all of these things to prepare my heart for a special day.

The service that day began with very earnest and heartfelt prayers. The congregation sang the wonderful old hymns with gusto. Then a hush fell over the assembly as the kindly pastor slowly made his way to the pulpit, placed his well-worn Bible there, and opened it to the passage of Scripture that God had impressed upon his heart to share. He then began to preach the powerful message, just as God gave it to him. He told us how we are all sinners and deserve to pay for our sins, but thankfully he didn't stop there. The preacher also told us about the great love that God has for us and how God sent His only Son, Jesus Christ, to die on an old, rugged cross, so that *we* wouldn't have to die for those sins. He told about a wonderful place called heaven that God had prepared for us. Heaven was so real, it seemed to me as if I could hear the angels singing. As he told us about an awful place called hell, the smell of brimstone seemed to fill my nose.

This particular day, it seemed that every word preached was meant just for me. I was leaning forward in the pew, listening intently, so as not to miss a single word. My heart was beating faster and faster as I listened to the message. As I sat on the edge of my seat, I lost sight of everybody else in the congregation, and that old, gray-haired preacher man seemed to be replaced by Jesus Himself! With His arms outstretched, a wonderful love seemed to flow from His eyes to mine as it drew me closer and closer. Jesus asked if He could come into my heart. A sweet, warm glow surrounded me as I realized my need to make a personal decision about my eternal destiny. I was not able to sit there quietly any longer. I jumped to my feet, literally ran all the way to the altar, and fell on my knees. Tears of joy streamed down my face. The most wonderful peace that I'd ever experienced then flooded my soul! Joy indescribable washed over me.

A little boy of a tender age said, "Yes, Lord Jesus, yes!"

At this time, I also knew that God was calling me to preach the gospel. However, it was many years later that I actually answered that call.

"For God so loved the world that he gave his only begotten Son, that whosoever believeth on him should not perish, but have everlasting life" (John 3:16).

Christmas Time

Christmas is supposed to be a day of celebration of the birth of Jesus Christ, and for the Daileys, the focus of the holidays definitely *was* about Jesus. In retrospect, being of limited means does have its benefits. Without all the commercial distractions that we now have, we were taught the true meaning of Christmas. So much is lost in the glitz and the moneymaking business of today. With so much to do, so many places to go, and so many presents to buy, often Christ is completely left out of Christmas. As children, we listened as the account of the birth of Jesus was read from the Bible. We sang Christmas carols, went to church, and watched or participated in plays about the story of Jesus' birth.

As in many households, it was a Dailey family tradition to cut down a pretty cedar tree and bring it into the house. We'd prop the tree up in a bucket with rocks piled around the trunk, and cover the bucket with an old bedsheet. The fragrance of the fresh-cut cedar made the house smell wonderful. Mom would cook popcorn, and we all helped to string it before draping the strings on the branches. We would cut out paper ornaments, stars, and angels, and decorate our tree as a crackling fire kept us warm. The smell of the wood burning in the fireplace permeated the air as the family sang carols. Just the thought of the fragrance of Mom's scrumptious cookies baking in the wood stove makes my mouth water, even to this day.

On Christmas morning, we would each get an apple and an orange in a little brown paper bag. If it was a very good year, we would each get a stick of peppermint candy also.

Although our family did not have much by the world's standards, by our own personal standards, we were very rich indeed. We had faith in

God and knew that with God, all things were possible. We had each other, and yes, there were lots of "Merry Christmas" wishes shared by all!

Aside from a brown paper bag of fruit and a rare stick of peppermint, the first conventional Christmas gift I ever received was given to me when I was about twelve years old. It was an exciting day when my older brother, who had been working up north, came home for the holidays. He brought me a cap pistol. I thought I was really something, running around the yard, shooting up the place. Our dog was missing for several days after that. He'd never heard such a commotion!

"For unto you is born this day in the city of David a Savior, which is Christ the Lord.

And this shall be a sign unto you, ye shall find the babe wrapped in swaddling clothes, lying in a manger." (Luke 2:11–12)

Everyday Stuff

The winter months found the family setting traps for critters. If we could trap it or shoot it, Mom would cook it, and we'd have a feast! Rabbits, birds, groundhogs, and squirrels were all in danger with the Daileys in the woods. I was pretty good at whittling slingshots out of forked limbs. Birds and rabbits, be wary or be dinner!

Raindrops pitter-pattering on the old tin roof and a deep featherbed made for the best sleep a feller ever had, after a long day of work and play. Before school each day, we would always check the traps. One morning, to our misfortune, we found we had caught a skunk! No matter how carefully one may try to avoid it, that awful smell has a way of getting on you and hanging on. Sorta like a hair in a biscuit! It makes no difference how many lye soap baths or home remedies one may try; nothing beats the passage of time for getting rid of that stink. And my goodness, how *slowly* time crawls along when kids are laughing at you!

When I was thirteen years old, I worked many odd jobs for neighbors and saved all my money in an old fruit jar. It took every penny I had saved to pay five dollars for a used bike. Bear in mind that five dollars was a *lot* of money back then. You would have thought I'd just bought a new Cadillac, as proud as I was of that bicycle! I rode it around those Tennessee hills for years. I wasn't satisfied with my speed until all you could see was a huge dust ball rolling behind me, as I pedaled my bike down that dirt road as fast as I could go. "Yeee-ha!" Kinda reminds me of a friend who declared that he was going at least ninety miles an hour on his old bike. I don't think I was going *quite* that fast, though! Those are some really good memories.

We'd practice "baptizing" the chickens and cats. Then we graduated to baptizing each other. The older boys nearly drowned Donald and me, because we were the scrawniest of the bunch.

Splashing in the creek, skipping stones on the surface of the pond, and playing jokes on each other filled our summers—that is, after we finished with each day's chores. Feeding the chickens, slopping the hogs, or getting the cows up took a lot of our time. On those hot summer days, there was still time to drown a few worms at the nearest pond. We called it fishing with a cane pole. Now *that* was really fun, watching the cork first bob and then disappear under the water's surface. We just never knew what was on the other end of that line! On a good day we were proud little tykes, and took home a mess of fresh fish for supper.

Many hot summer evenings would find us sitting around the porch, shelling peas, snapping beans, or running around the yard catching lightning bugs in old fruit jars.

Aunt Mandy lived down the road just a little ways from our house. She was always a welcome visitor, and she loved to tell us stories. This is just one reason why Mandy was a favorite aunt and was loved by everybody who knew her. Many times, she would spend the night with us, and we always looked forward to her visits. She was one of the *best* at spinning those tall tales. Aunt Mandy reminded me of Granny on *The Beverly Hillbillies*. When she'd start a story, in no time at all, she had us spellbound, hearts racing, and lips a-quivering. We would see just who could scrunch the closest to her as she left us yearning for more. Then she'd go tuck us in those deep featherbeds. We would all be huddling close together, to keep the *boogers* from getting one of us.

The fall air carried on the wind the fragrance of burning leaves and pumpkin pies. The amber glow of the setting sun was indeed the perfect ambiance for the end of a pleasant autumn day. It seemed that no time at all passed before the fireplace was roaring and the snow was flying, drifting down in beautiful clumps, clinging to the trees, and creating a winter wonderland. It was wonderful—*until* we had to go out in it to get the firewood, brush off all that snow, and stomp our feet on the porch, so none of it would mess up Mom's clean floors.

I remember our family was the first in the community to acquire a battery-powered radio. After a long day's work, just as the sun was setting, many of our neighbors came from miles around, gathered on the front porch, and even spilled out into the yard to listen quietly to the Friday night broadcast of the Grand Old Opry. I still remember just how special that felt. Many people came from quite far just to listen to that radio. Not a single one of Mom's flowers was trampled on; nor did anybody make a mess. There was just a politeness and genuine respect that both children and adults had towards each other back then.

Many years later, my good friends Harold and Barbara Pannell invited my wife Thelma and me to go with them to the Grand Old Opry in Nashville, Tennessee. What a thrill that was for us! We even had the privilege to go backstage and meet several of the singers. Later, Billy Walker (one of the Opry singers) and his wife Betty became clients of mine at my vitamin and herb store. A few months later they came to the church that I pastored, Swallows Chapel in Rickman, Tennessee. Billy preached and sang, to the delight of our church. Only a very short time later, God called them both home to be with Him.

Howard with friends Harold and Barbara Pannell

Harold also took us to Dollywood in Pigeon Forge, Tennessee, to hear his good friend and Grand Old Opry star Jean Shepherd perform. Later we had the privilege to eat lunch and talk with Jean and her husband Bennie. We considered that to be quite an honor to visit with such delightful people.

Another time, Harold, who is quite a "man about town," brought a world-champion boxer to our Wednesday night church service. He had never been knocked out (in the ring, anyway), until that night. As I laid hands on him and began to pray, he fell straight backwards under the power of the Holy Spirit. He was bewildered and wondered what in the world had just happened to him. People who have never seen this occur might ask why, when you pray for people, do they sometimes *fall?* I once heard a minister describe it this way: when the presence and power of the Holy Spirit touches you in such a powerful way, if you can't *float,* you will *fall.* He fell. He had never had that kind of experience before. He wasn't expecting a little country preacher's praying to have such an impact on his life. It certainly wasn't me but the Holy Spirit working through me. To God be the glory!

Mom

My words do not do justice to Mom. She was one of a kind, a wonderful, caring, loving mother to us all. Mom and Dad were married when she was only thirteen years old, and they were married for seventy-two years. They loved God first, each other, and us, thus setting a beautiful example of what a marriage was supposed to be like. Their love for each other and for all of us prepared us for the love of our heavenly Father.

Ermine and Newton Dailey (Howard's mom and dad)

My earliest memories are of Mom rocking me. She loved to rock her babies, and we loved it too. As a child, I remember being sick many times. Every time I'd awaken, she would be right there by my bed, wiping my brow with a wet cloth, trying to keep my fever down. The comforting sound of her soft humming would put me right back to sleep. When *she* slept, I'll never know. She was always there for us, day or night.

The lingering fragrance of her homemade biscuits, mingled with smells from the wood-burning stove, awoke me in the early mornings. Afternoons might find sweet potatoes, ham, and redeye gravy cooking. Many times when food was scarce, we would have beans and cornbread; then, just to change things up a bit, sometimes we'd switch and have cornbread and beans! Food often became thin in wintertime, but God always provided. These events evoke such powerful memories.

I can still see Mom standing at the kitchen door, wearing one of her gingham aprons, wiping the sweat from her face, and calling us home for supper.

Like all families, we had problems, but Mom always prayed to see us through. When we had a particular problem, we knew we could always go to her and she'd pray. She always prayed for us before we left home.

A mother's prayer for her child is the stuff of lifelong memories. Mom would slip into our room at night, kneel at the foot of our beds, and pray specifically for each one of us. That would either make for sweet sleep, or if conviction came, one might lie there squirming all night long!

Mom gave my brother Robert a New Testament just before he left to serve in the Korean War. He carried it in his shirt pocket all the time. He literally heard Momma's prayers when he was in a foxhole. Even though he wasn't a Christian at that time, he *knew* it was Momma's prayers that brought him safely home. Robert has since given his heart to God and is one of the *giants* in the Lord. A mightier prayer warrior this world seldom sees; he'd rather pray for somebody than eat—yet another answer to one of Mom and Dad's prayers.

Robert (Bob) Dailey – one of Howard's brothers. Photo by Barbara Pannell

After spending a lifetime on their knees praying, Mom and Dad were assured by God that *all* their children would be saved.

Looking back at these times, and now being a parent myself, it really gives my heart a great big tug.

Dad

One autumn day, my dad started getting sick. He was about fifty-five years of age at the time. As he became sicker and sicker, he went back and forth to the doctors many times, and they ran tests of all sorts. The doctors told us he had cancer of the stomach, and it was too far advanced to successfully treat. "Sorry, but that's all we can do." They sent him home with only a short time to live. Dad lost so much weight that he appeared to be only skin and bones, but we never gave up hope of his recovery. When Dad could no longer attend church with us, he would always remind us to ask the elders to come to the house, anoint him with oil, and pray for him. Time after time, we would ask them to pray, and they would always come. We would gather around his bed, anoint him with oil—just like it says in the Bible—and pray.

"Is any sick among you? Let him call for the elders of the church, and let them pray over him, anointing him with oil in the name of the Lord:

And the prayer of faith shall save the sick, and the Lord shall raise him up ...

... The effectual fervent prayer of a righteous man availeth much."

(James 5:14–16)

With Dad sick, there came the time when we were no longer able to work the dairy farm, and so we had to move. Times were very hard. We kept praying that one day Dad would be healed, but his body grew very weak and frail.

Twenty-two Pennies

During this very difficult time in our lives, we kept going to church, praying, and asking everybody we knew to pray. We kept the faith, even when it appeared we had nothing to hang on to. God is faithful, always faithful.

One particular Sunday I will never forget. We were all lined up in our pew as usual. Dad being too sick to go with us to church made it that much more important for us to go. What I didn't understand at the time was that when they passed the offering plate, Mom put her offering in as usual. However, on this Sunday, it was *all* the money we had in the world—all twenty-two cents. What was she thinking? But she knew the Scriptures.

She knew that the Bible said to give and it shall be given to you. She knew that one cannot outgive the Lord. She knew that when a person has a desperate need, he or she must give. So she gave her all.

It was a gentle tug on a small boy's heart.

"Bring ye all the tithes into the storehouse, that there may be meat in mine house, and prove me now herewith, saith the Lord of hosts, if I will not open you the windows of heaven, and pour you out a blessing, that there shall not be room enough to receive it." (Malachi 3:10)

These were very hard times, and food was hard to come by. One day, before daybreak, a farmer in a big flatbed truck came rolling down our dusty dirt road. He knocked on our front door and said, "Morning, Mrs. Dailey. I have several fields of strawberries that are rotting with nobody to pick them." He had heard that we had a big family with a bunch of kids. He asked if she and all the kids would like to help him. Would we! We were a hungry bunch, not even knowing where our next meal was coming from. Yes, we were tickled to be able to work. Mom got us all up, we quickly got dressed, and out the door we all went. We all piled in the back of his truck, and he drove us out to his strawberry fields.

We picked strawberries all day long. First we'd pick two and eat two, and then we'd pick two and eat one. Finally we began to put them all in the bucket. They were the best, sweetest strawberries we had ever eaten.

At the end of the day, the farmer asked, "Mrs. Dailey, how do you want me to pay the kids?" She told him to pay each one of us for what we did. He paid us; we then gave all of the money to Mom. On the way home, the farmer was nice enough to stop by the country grocery store. That money bought lots of groceries for some hungry children. God still provides.

Another gentle tug on a small boy's heart.

In a few months, Dad started getting better. He first started sitting up a little and then going out onto the porch. Soon he ventured out into the yard a little bit, getting more sun and fresh air with each passing day. He became progressively better and soon was working a full day. One day, all tan and healthy, he went into town. The doctor saw him and was astonished, as the doctors had expected him to die. The doctor said, "Mr. Dailey, you look so good! What did *we* do to make you well?"

Dad said, "You didn't do anything. You sent me home to die. God healed me!" Dad lived to be almost ninety-six years old. Isn't God good!

Yet another gentle tug on a small boy's heart.

Tadpoles and Marbles

Little boys eventually grow up, leaving the tadpoles and marbles far behind. They start thinking about the birds and the bees. In those days, we started combing our hair with a kind of swirl; some people used to call it a "duck tail." To be really cool, we would stand our collars up, and we even starched a crease in our jeans.

My friends and I heard about a revival prayer meeting that was going on in town, so we went. It was a hot summer, and we knew that the windows would be open so we could check out the girls without ever going inside. At that time, we thought that was pretty slick.

Howard about 16 years old   Thelma about 16 years old

The visiting minister was from way up north, a place called Michigan. We heard he had a real pretty daughter. Sure enough, one look and I was smitten! She had the prettiest blue eyes I had ever seen. The guys all told me she was a city slicker and that she wouldn't have anything to do with me. I told them to "hide and watch." I also told them that the next night I'd be sitting there right beside her. They said, "No way." Soon, with all the commotion going on outside the window, sure enough she looked my way; and with the biggest irresistible smile I could muster, I put a big ol' wink on her. To my amazement, she smiled back! I went around to the front door and waited for church to dismiss. Eventually she came out. With sweaty palms and my heart all a-flutter, I managed to seem real cool and talked to her. I guess it was fate. Sure enough, the next night, there I sat, proud as a peacock. We visited several times during that week. I went back and told the boys, "That's the girl of my dreams. I'm going to marry her." Again, laughing at me, they said, "No way." I again said, "You'll see."

At the end of the week, my heart broke when she had to go back to Michigan with her parents. We wrote letters back and forth for the whole next year. She came back the following summer with her parents, who were holding another revival at the same church. At age seventeen, I had already decided she really was the one I wanted to spend my whole life with. I asked her to marry me, and to my surprise, she said yes.

Next we had to talk to her parents. They wouldn't even *hear* anything about such a crazy thing as our getting married. After all, we were both *only* seventeen. We were just kids, without even a job! They knew that love alone doesn't pay bills. I lived at home with my parents and was only earning money by doing odd jobs for the neighbors. They did agree to our going to a movie instead. Okay, so we'd go to a movie. Change of plans. So, with the help of my sister Beulah, we eloped.

Upon our return, it was my job to break the news to her family. I timidly knocked on the door. After telling her mother that we had gotten married, she slammed the door right in my face! With sheer determination I glumly sat down on the front steps, elbows resting on knees, chin pressing into sweaty palms, until her father came home. He wasn't exactly happy with our decision either, but he said, "Okay, *you* married her, *you* take care of her." We packed her belongings and went to live with my folks for a few months until we could get on our feet. Now I have a much better understanding of the reasoning behind their reaction. There stood a "still wet behind the ears" kid, who had only known his daughter for basically two weeks (not counting the time we wrote back and forth), and he wanted to marry their daughter. How absurd!

My wife Thelma, being the glamorous city girl, was much more accustomed to painting her nails and styling her hair than she was to the chores of country life. She didn't quite know what to think about gathering the eggs, slopping the hogs, or wringing a chicken's neck. Some days, she wasn't even sure she still lived in the United States! From the fashion magazines to the chicken coops was quite a stretch for a city girl, but she made it. Thankfully, we soon moved to Michigan to live in a basement apartment at her Mom and Dad's house. At that time I started working as a laborer, building chain-link fences.

Having just arrived from way down South, more than once I was teased for saying, "Thank you, thank you very much," in a very distinct Southern drawl. I'd blush when they asked me if I was kin to Elvis. Why, I thought everybody talked liked that!

Howard (a proud new daddy!) holding Tina

Soon, babies started arriving. Our first child was born one year after we were married, in 1962. We named her Tina. I was so excited that I walked right through a plate-glass door at the hospital and managed to get a six-inch gash in my thigh. I also managed to make the next day's headlines in the paper: "Proud father walks through plate-glass door."

One year later, our son Bruce made his appearance in July 1963. Thankfully, this time wasn't quite so dramatic. Two years later, our third child Lonnie was born. He was to be the caboose on the baby train.

The Dailey family. Left to right; Thelma, Howard, Lonnie, Tina and Bruce

We started going to the Freewill Baptist Church, mostly because my father-in-law was a Baptist minister, and he was a really big man! Just kidding. It was because I wanted my children raised in church. After a proving time, my in-laws and I became good friends and grew to respect each other. They were very good to us.

Was that ... another tug?

After years of seeing my parents strive so hard to put food on the table, I was determined that my family would not have life as hard as I did growing up.

I managed to secure good jobs, even though the ability to perform them normally required a lot more formal education than I actually had. At the time, I attributed it to grit, grin, and pure determination. Not until several years later did I realize that it was the hand of God all along.

It wasn't long after being away from my roots that I slowly started drifting away from living the life that I should have been living, even though I was still attending church.

Tug ... what tug?

Now, What Was That Request?

This period of my life is not one I'm proud of. It is important, however, to show just how very powerful intercessory prayers are for our loved ones. Also, I believe we are who we are today because of all the combined seasons of our lives.

While living in Michigan, Thelma, the kids, and I, often came down to Tennessee to visit my family for a few days. One particular time while there, my brothers and I were going places we should not have been going and doing things that we should not have been doing. I'll skip the finer details, and only say that looking at pretty women is what young men like to do. My brothers had been drinking, but that wasn't my thing, so I was the designated driver in this escapade. We were heading out of town in a fancy sports car. A frisky-looking bunch, we thought we were. With a fresh splash of good-smelling aftershave and one last peek in the mirror to make sure I looked as good as I felt, we were off and running. At the time, Brylcreem was high fashion. We all had our hair slicked back, gleaming with the stuff, and of course the shirt collars were all turned up. Were we *hot* or what?

I reached for the dial on the radio and turned it, trying to find some good music to drown out my nagging conscience and get my mind off what we were going out to do. However, as I was spinning that dial, something caught my breath in midair. I paused on a particular station just long enough to realize it was a gospel music station that was taking call-in prayer requests. *What—is that Momma's voice I hear?* Shivers went down my spine as I heard her specific prayer request was for me! "I've got three boys out there, and I know they're doing something that they should not be doing. Especially Howard."

That's all it took. With a loud screech, I locked that car down, right smack in the middle of the road. I spun it around and took my brothers back to their cars before they even had time to wonder what in the world had just happened. I headed straight back to the house, humiliated. Talking about feathers falling or a bad puppy dog with his tail tucked between his legs; that was *exactly* the way I felt.

It was *really* hard pulling into the driveway, slowly opening the car door, and walking up to the house, knowing that Mom already knew. I *knew* better. I also knew that my mom was so tuned in to God's voice, not much *ever* escaped her.

Mom met me at the door. All she said was, "Son, I've been praying for you."

I hung my head even lower. "I know."

It was a firm tug on a young man's heart. A heart that *knew* better. You can throw the first rock if you've never done anything wrong.

"He that is without sin among you, let him first cast a stone." (John 8:7)

In spite of myself, God would use me in a profound way.

God, Are You Sure?

There truly is no justification for half-heartedly serving the Lord, but in reality, that was exactly what I was doing during this time of my life. God had His hand on me, and He was not about to give up, even if I was reluctant to obey.

When my older brother Robert asked me to go to a Nashville hospital to be with his family as they took his mother-in-law off life support, neither Robert nor his wife were Christians. Her mom, a very sweet lady, had leukemia and cirrhosis of the liver. Every vein in her body had already collapsed, and her organs had shut down. She had been through a lot of suffering and pain. It seemed that her time on this Earth was just about over.

They had disconnected her from life support by the time I arrived. The doctor had already officially pronounced her dead.

The saddened family was standing all around her bed. Then God spoke to me and told me to lay hands on her.

Who, *me*?

I just stood there. He spoke once again to go lay hands on her.

I'm thinking, *God, she's already dead.* (As if He didn't know that.)

Again, God said for me to go lay hands on her.

God, are you sure?

Silence. I reluctantly obeyed and slowly walked over to her bed.

Did I feel unworthy? You bet I did. Did I feel foolish? You bet I did. Did I wonder what *they* thought? You bet I did. Did God care what I thought? Not on your life. God just wants our obedience.

With my eyes closed—whether in reverence or fear I don't know—I laid my hands on her. It felt like a bolt of lightning went straight through me! The kids started screaming, "Mama, Mama!"

She opened her eyes, looked around, and said, "Raise my bed up. You know I don't like to sleep with my head down."

With all the commotion that was going on, the doctor came running back into the room. What he saw as he pushed the door open startled him. He was *sure* he had seen a ghost. White as a sheet, *he* was the one who looked more like a ghost.

They kept her in the hospital for a few days longer to run tests. Everything checked normal. She lived twenty-eight more wonderful years! I had the privilege of holding her funeral all those years later.

"They shall lay hands on the sick, and they shall recover." (Mark 16:18)

"Verily, verily, I say unto you, He that believeth on me, the works that I do shall he do also; and greater works than these shall he do; because I go unto my Father." (John 14:12)

Bad to the Bone

After first building fences, I then got a job in a machine shop as a laborer but was promoted to a press operator within a few days. I quickly moved on to become a tool-and-die maker. Next, my family moved to Monroe, Michigan, where I would help build nuclear power plants. I worked as a supervisor over warehousing and truck drivers. Working with a lot of bullies and rough guys, I figured I gotta be tough just to survive. I got myself two single-bladed Boker knives. I practiced and practiced until my movements were as smooth as silk, very quick, which seemed almost effortless.

I could pull those knives out simultaneously, so fast that people thought they were switchblades. I always carried those knives with me for protection. I had to at least project the image that I was "bad to the bone" or that rough bunch of men would have had me for breakfast!

The power plant was a tough place to work, and everybody knew that I also carried a gun. I'd take it out and put it in the locker as soon as I got to work. There was one particular guy who was notorious for harassing me. Every day, he got more and more aggressive. He'd come by me, flipping my hardhat off and pulling my hair. It wasn't just me; he had a habit of aggravating just about everybody who worked there. On one particular day, I'd had just about enough of him. I told him that one day I was going to have my gun with me and kill him. What he didn't know was that I had a blank pistol that looked just like the real thing.

The next night when the bully came by and flipped everybody's hardhats off, I was ready for him. I immediately pulled out my gun, loaded with blanks, and "shot" him. It being dark, the blaze of fire that came out of the gun looked like the real deal. It scared that man even more than

I'd dared to hope for. He fell right over in the floor. Then he popped up and ran all the way to first aid, thinking he was dying. I was right behind him, running as fast as I could, yelling at him, trying my best to tell him it was only a blank. The first-aid people quickly took his clothes off to see where he'd been shot. Feeling very foolish, I explained that it was only a blank. Still they didn't believe me, until I turned the gun on myself and shot, to prove it wasn't real. There was no more hat flipping after that night, though, and I got a lot more respect. By word of mouth, all the new people were told, "Don't mess with Dailey. Dailey will kill you!"

Next to the nuclear power plant was a trailer for my office, with thirty drivers working under my supervision. I always got there first. The drivers came in and reported to me every morning.

One particular morning, some of the drivers arrived before I did. They slipped into the trailer and filled my hardhat with Gojo, which is a gritty hand-cleaning liquid.

The first thing I'd do each day was put the hardhat on, go out, and see what jobs needed to be done. This particular morning I put it on, and all that goo came running down my face. The very same moment, the guys who had come up with this joke came through the door at precisely the right time to see it happening. The biggest guy came in first. As I flung the hardhat off, the goo-filled hat hit him squarely in the chest. The force of it knocked him back out the door, and five more guys came in right behind him. I reached behind me and came up with a two-by-four, and soon all six were laid out on the ground. Some drivers came up—after the fact—to see if I needed any help. "Nope, taken care of." I figured I'd surely be fired after all of that, but it didn't happen. I did earn the respect of the crew for the duration of this job.

When this job was completed, I tried driving OTR (over-the-road) in an eighteen-wheeler, but soon tired of being away from home so much, so I went back to the same machine shop where I'd worked previously. As a rule, the union would not allow the company to hire a person back in the same position that he had left, but somehow I was allowed to return. Rehiring for the same position was unheard of, but the hand of God was definitely in this as well. I was able to repair a machine in about one hour that had sat idle for weeks. It was broken and nobody thus far was able to fix it.

Sometimes I felt a gentle tug; other times I *thought* I was just plain tough.

God Calling Me

We left Michigan in 1975 and moved back to Tennessee. I missed my friends, family, and all those beautiful Tennessee hills. I thought it would be a wonderful environment to raise my family.

I bought a service station in Hilham, Tennessee. We called it Dailey's Car Care Center. Everything was going well; business was growing, and I loved it. At this time, my family and I were attending Fairview Freewill Baptist Church in Livingston, Tennessee. For three straight weeks, God relentlessly chased me to answer His call to preach the gospel.

Not being ready, I resisted His call. I wasn't able to sleep. On a Tuesday at 12:30 AM, I was sitting in the family room, just thinking while everybody else was sleeping.

God spoke to me in my spirit: *"Go preach My gospel."*

I said, "God, if that is You speaking, have somebody call me right now." Immediately the phone rang.

"It's Dad," the voice said. "Hasn't God called you to preach?"

Filled with emotion, I couldn't talk at length. I said, "Dad, I love you. I'll talk to you later."

Things at home hadn't been going very well. Most families go through these things every once in a while, but lately we were constantly at each other's throats and neither one of us would back down, making life almost unbearable.

The following Tuesday night after a long hard day at work, my wife and the kids decided to go shopping, and I had grudgingly been coerced into going. On the way home we got into a "big fuss." I was tired, sore, and didn't want to be there in the first place, so I'm sure I was just a little bit short. I guess I was trying to make her mad enough to leave me. Right in the heat of the argument, I heard that same voice, *"Go preach my gospel."*

If that's you speaking, God, let somebody else say something about me preaching.

Upset from all the commotion, the kids were crying. My son Bruce reached over the car seat and said, "Dad, one day you're going to make a great preacher."

A sharp stab in the heart of a grown man.

The following Tuesday, the pastor of our church had asked me and another church member to meet with a man about buying a new heating and cooling unit for our sanctuary. The pastor thought I had good business sense, and may could get a better price, so he elected me for the meeting. I willingly accepted. The company representative was running a little late, so the other member and I were chatting. We decided to give him five more minutes; if he hadn't shown up by then, we would leave.

That same voice spoke to me once again: *"Go preach my gospel."*

The other brother waiting with me said, "Brother Dailey, I've got something I've been meaning to ask you. Hasn't God called you to preach?"

Another tug to my heart.

I told the man that we would have to talk about this later. Thankfully, the repairman finally showed up. I asked the repairman for an estimate, and he gave us one, which was way over the amount we knew we could spend. He reluctantly agreed to a lesser amount and even said he didn't know why he was doing this job for so little money.

So with that job taken care of, I left to go home. God had a distinct call on my life. I was totally miserable and didn't know what to do about it. I guess I was too stubborn to totally say yes to God *just yet.*

If God calls you to serve Him,

Don't miss the call the first time around.

Don't flinch,

Don't duck.

If God chases you, He's sure to win.

He runs fastest!

God's Not Looking for Perfect People

He certainly wouldn't have called me if He were! God is looking for real people who will be obedient to His call. We are *real* people living in a *real* world, with *real* problems. But we have a *real* God that's a problem solver.

Questions – Questions

I had a great business, making money head over heels. I was well on my way to becoming rich, just as I'd promised myself. My family would not have it as hard as I had growing up, but still I wasn't happy. Questions, lots of questions, began to run through my head; I was confused. The world had lots to offer. Did I marry too young? What had I done or not done? Was I missing something? With so much responsibility of family, business, and church, there were lots of things I had not experienced. I was an emotional train wreck waiting to happen. Frustrated!

After silently pondering the options for quite some time, I finally made up my mind: I'd run away. I had a lot of cash in hand, and I went looking for somebody to run away with. I'd start a new life someplace else with a new identity. I'd go where nobody would find me, not even God!

Would you believe I couldn't even find anybody who was interested in running away with me? What an ego buster!

Then, once again, God said, *"I've got you. You've got to preach my gospel."*

I Give Up

Okay, Lord, I give up! I repent. Cleanse me, make me a person fit to preach your gospel. Anoint me. Fill me with your Holy Spirit.

It felt like my car drove home all by itself.

I told Thelma and the kids that they had to repent also. Everything became like new to me. I preached to everything and everybody. I preached to my wife, my kids, and the walls. The dog even got a sermon that day. I took a shower and nearly preached the curtain off. To this day, I still get a lot of my messages while I'm taking a shower.

After I got out of the shower and quickly dried off, I called one of my brothers and told him that he had to repent or he'd go to hell. He asked me if I was drunk, even though he *knew* I didn't drink. My brother hung up on me, but he called me right back. "Are you serious? Well, come on over and talk to us." So, about 11:00 PM, I went to their house. Several members of my family were saved that night.

Then, about 12:30 AM, I called my pastor and told him I'd answered the call to preach. He said, "Good. Would you like to preach tonight?" This was on a Wednesday night.

"Well, yes, I guess I would."

All day, I called people on the phone and told them that God had called me to preach the gospel, that God had forgiven my sins and cleaned me up. I invited them to hear me preach at the service that night.

At church that night, knowing that I was to be the main speaker, I sat on the front row. Being the flashy dresser that I've always been known to be, I wore my bright red blazer. As I read my Bible, pondering the Scripture that I had been reading, I was oblivious to the growing crowd that had gathered behind me. The pastor stood up and said, "We have a surprise tonight. Howard is going to preach."

I got up, turned around, and saw that the house was completely packed. This was very unusual. Immediately my knees started bumping together like marbles in a sock! Even though I had invited a lot of people, I never dreamed that so many of them would show up!

I will never forget the message that I preached that night. It's found in Luke 16:19–25. "The Rich Man and Lazarus" was the title of my first sermon.

God gave me this particular message especially for this night. I saw people dying and going to hell, but they didn't have to go there. Their sin debt had already been paid. People go to hell because they are rejecting what Jesus had already paid for. Everybody must make their own personal decision about their future.

Several people repented of their sins. Many came down to the altar and were saved. It was an exciting first night of preaching God's Word!

About three months later, I was called to pastor Fairview Freewill Baptist Church in Livingston, Tennessee.

Soon after this time in my life, several different churches started calling me for meetings, revivals, and camp meetings. At the same, time I was running my new business. Life was going at a very fast pace.

God's Way

There is a song that several people have recorded called "My Way." You may remember that Elvis, as well as many others, sang it.

Well, I tried "My Way," but God has a way of making one very miserable until one does it *His* way.

In 1977, I was a mere thirty-two years old. One might say I was living the American Dream. I was a working man, married to a beautiful lady and raising three wonderful children. It seemed I had everything except the white picket fence. I owned a car-care business, in which I totally enjoyed working on vehicles and interacting with the customers. I was also pastoring a small church at that time, which I also *knew* I was called to do. On the outside, all looked well, but on the inside, I was troubled.

Growing discontentment, unsettling thoughts, and turmoil soured my life. Spiritual warfare whirled through my head. Sometimes I wasn't even completely aware that it was there—somewhat like the wind blowing the leaves in a tree; you know it's there, but where does it come from?

For three consecutive nights prior to the horrible motorcycle accident, I had dreams, one in which I saw my own death. (Yes, that was my motorcycle in the introduction to this book. I was the one the hearse had come to collect.) Not knowing what I should or should not do about those dreams, I kept it all to myself.

There's a story I heard about a little boy traveling with his mother by car, obviously before the seat belt law. He kept standing up when he should have been sitting down. After being told for the third time, he finally sat down. Arms crossed, lips poked out, under his breath his mother heard him say, "But I'm standing up *inside*."

On the outside, I was doing all the right things, but on the inside I was "standing up."

Dreams

Our small community kept growing. My car-care business was growing and growing. I had six or seven employees working for me at any one time.

After several months of working all day and preaching at night, I started turning down requests to preach, in order to work more. It's so easy to get our focus "off." Mine was on more money. I wanted to be rich, and I was well on my way.

My wife, two of our three children, and my mother had gone to Michigan for a much-needed vacation. They went there to visit Thelma's parents for a few days. My dad—being blind at this time—needed someone to stay with him around the clock. Beulah stayed with him during the day, and we both stayed with him at night.

During this week, I was holding a revival that had started on a Wednesday night. Each night after I finished preaching, I'd go over and spend the night at my dad's house.

I was awakened at 3:00 AM by a very vivid dream. I could hear a man shouting, "Howard, I made it!" The man was standing in front of me, dressed in a white robe. The most beautiful glow surrounded him. This was a man I had worked with many years ago in Michigan at the machine shop. I had witnessed to him and led him to the Lord. Two weeks later, the man had come down with cancer and died.

I immediately jumped out of bed after having this bad dream and could not go back to sleep. I just stayed up and went on in to work early.

I worked all day Thursday and went back to church that night for another night of revival. Then, after the service, I went back to my dad's house. Being very tired, I went on to bed.

Again I was awakened at 3:00 Friday morning with yet another very vivid dream. This time, I heard an awful, blood-curdling scream: *"Don't come into this place! Don't come into this place!"* I heard the awful sounds echoing out of a deep pit. I saw the outer darkness and heard the screams. I recognized his voice as a man I worked with at the power plant in Michigan. I had talked to him about the Lord, but he just made fun of what I said. Some of the workers sneeringly called me "deacon." One day while at work, sitting at a job conference, the man just suddenly fell over dead. He was a young man, in his early forties. I learned then that one does not have to be old to die, just alive.

The first man gave his heart to God. He was in a very beautiful place. The second one had rejected God. He was in a horrific place.

Heart racing, beads of sweat forming on my forehead, still shaken by this last dream, I jumped out of bed, horrified. I could not go back to sleep, so again I went in to work quite early.

I worked all day Friday and preached again on the third night of revival. On this particular night, God gave me a *special* message for the final night of this revival.

"The wicked shall be turned into hell, and all the nations that forget God." (Psalm 9:17)

"The Heavenly Dove Singers" One of the groups that traveled with Howard. Left to right; Sammy Neal, Howard and Thelma Dailey, Carolyn Hill, Jewell Bilbrey, Adam Hill and Jed Stevens.

I was blessed to have a group of faithful singers who traveled with me to the different churches. They sang a song that night called "Where the Roses Never Fade." We sang it once, and then it was requested that we sing it a second time. Just as we started to close the service, another lady requested that it be sung yet a third time. At this time, many people started flocking to the altar. We had more responses on this particular night than all the other nights put together.

When our group boarded the bus to go back home, I told the singers that if anything ever happened to me, I wanted them to sing that song at my funeral.

After services on that Friday night, I once again went back to my dad's house to spend the night. At 3:00 AM, I was awakened by another very bad dream. This time I saw my own death. I heard an audible voice say, *"This is death."*

Startled by this voice, I saw my own dead body in a casket. Lots of people were standing around. They were having my funeral. Then I saw them wheeling my casket out of the church to load it into the hearse. They would soon be on the way to the cemetery.

A woman said, "Oh no! He can't be dead! Let me see him one more time."

They opened the coffin. I heard God say, *"I'm performing a miracle. I'm letting you live."*

Horrified, I jumped out of bed. It felt like my heart was beating out of my chest. Sweat was pouring off my face.

I tried to slip quietly out of the house unnoticed, because I *had* to be alone. Beulah heard my fumbling around and insisted that she fix me some breakfast. I told her that I really didn't feel like eating. She wondered what was so wrong, because she knew how much I loved her cooking and still didn't want to eat. I told her I'd just had a very bad dream, and I went on to work.

This particular Saturday at work, there was an unusually large number of people who came by the shop to get work done, while others just wanted to talk. On June 11, 1977, there was a cloud of dreadful heaviness that hovered over me that I just couldn't seem to shake. It was a day that I will *never* forget.

Stranger in Town

The smell of grease, gas, and sweat permeated the hot summer air. I glanced up, and there against the sunlight I could make out the shadow of a man framed by the door; he had a long beard, scruffy clothes, and flip-flops. He was a stranger to these parts. The man made his way over to the counter and bought a small bag of peanuts and a soda, then he spotted my motorcycle and walked over to it.

I'd recently purchased a 1977 model 380 Suzuki racing bike. Having ridden bikes for seventeen years, I was immensely proud of this one. With all that power at my command, racing it gave me a rush. All my pent-up stress and frustration was just left to settle in the dust behind me. As the stranger's interest peaked in my bike, I couldn't help but ask, "Do you ride?"

"Yup," was his short reply. Just trying to make conversation, I asked, "You new to these parts?"

Again, a short response: "Just visiting."

Determined to get something more from him, I asked him, "Would you like to take it for a spin?"

"For real?" he asked, as he tried not to let on how excited he really was. I told him to go ahead. Pulling the keys off a rusty nail that hung by the door, I tossed them to the young man. With a big grin, he straddled the bike, fired it off, and gingerly maneuvered it around the station's traffic, and off he went.

He returned a couple hours later and parked it where he'd found it. "Looks good. Great ride, but there's something I just can't put my finger on. Something about that fork ain't quite right."

I thought about what the man said a brief moment, but I heard other customers who needed my attention, and off I went. Not till later did I even recall that event. I had never seen the man before, and I never saw him again afterward.

I had plenty of time to think about it later, though. Much too much time.

A young man who attended our church had bought a new motorcycle. He wanted to show it off and he wanted me to go for a ride with him. We were really busy, so I told him he'd have to wait until we caught up a little bit.

I spotted my sister-in-law Bennie at the gas pump getting a fill-up and went over to her. I said, "Bennie, if I don't see you anymore on this side, I'll see you in heaven."

"Aw, Howard, quit talking like that," was her reply.

When we got caught up, I told the young man that we could now go for that ride. As we went over to get our cycles, my older brother Herman walked over to us and said, "Don't go on this ride. You'll be killed. I have a bad feeling."

"I've ridden these cycles for seventeen years," I told him. "I'll be all right."

As we started to leave, I hadn't put my helmet on. Herman was watching me and yelled, "At least put your helmet on!" Reaching back, I grabbed it, hastily pulled it on, and snapped it in place.

We had planned to go on an eight-mile ride. About three miles into the ride, a strange feeling came over me. Feeling like I really should turn around and go back to the station, I made a motion to the other man to turn around. We started back. At less than a quarter mile, we came into a curve. Suddenly, something on my bike malfunctioned. The front wheel locked up, causing an abrupt screeching halt. The sudden stop propelled me through the air. My body hit a tree headfirst and slid upside down onto the ground. I landed headfirst in a crumpled, bloody heap amid the tall grass and weeds. I saw all this happen, seemingly in slow motion. As I hit the tree, I saw a very bright light surrounding me, and I heard a voice say, *"This is death."*

Immediately my spirit went out of my physical body. I quickly went through a bright light; I was then standing in the most beautiful place I have ever seen! Trying to take this in all at once, I noticed that there were flowers of all colors and shapes with the most wonderful fragrances one could ever imagine. There were trees and lush fields of grass in varying hues of green, many colors I have never even seen here on earth. I saw beautiful gardens and many different species of animals. Many people, some I had known on Earth and others I just seemed to know, came to welcome me. I noticed that they all had very youthful looks, with brilliant, glowing complexions. Everything I encountered was so very peaceful; the most tranquil place one could imagine. One might say *heavenly!*

The music seemed to be flowing from every direction at the same time. The voices and instruments intermingled so closely that it was impossible to distinguish one from another. I have never heard such wonderful harmony, deliciously blending together. There seemed to be no beginning or ending. Eternal, that's it—it felt eternal! Sometimes in very quite moments, I still seem to hear that beautiful heavenly music, sounds I long to hear again and know that one day I will. What a glorious thought!

At the very same time, I could see what was happening back on Earth. My body had hit a tree, and I was lying face down with my helmet still on. The young man who had been riding with me wheeled his bike around, frantically dismounted, and ran to my side. He paused, tenderly picked me up, and carried me in his arms to the edge of the road. After a pause he took my helmet off. "Oh no, he's dead!" he exclaimed with a trembling voice. By now there were people beginning to gather, standing all around the wreck. I saw my body lying on the ground. Beside me the young man knelt in a curled position, not knowing what to do. People stopped their vehicles and ran over to see the carnage. I was seeing this take place from a heavenly viewpoint, which is much different from anything I had ever experienced before.

A lady who had taken the same route we had came upon the wreck, jumped out of her car, rushed over to me, and checked me for any signs of life. With tears in her eyes, she said, "He's dead." She sat on the ground and cradled my head. She said that she would stay there while my friend went to get help. The young man jumped back on his bike and took off to the car-care station.

I could see the young man telling Herman that I was dead. I watched as they called for help on the phone. (This was before cell phones or even 911 in that area.)

At the same time, I could see other areas. Friends had gone to tell my dad about the accident. He was standing on the front porch, and he took the news very hard. I watched as they told my son Bruce and two other brothers and a brother-in-law, who were all working in a hot and dusty hay field.

Rumbling Down the Road
(Driver of the hearse)

The driver was more interested in the clock ticking closer to quitting time. He pushed his cap back, wiped the beads of sweat from off his forehead with the back of his hand, and with a firm tug pulled his cap back down on his head. He squinted toward the sun while thinking that the pastures were kind of dry for this time of year.

The old hearse rumbled down the dusty country road, slowing down to take the curves. The driver knew there was no need to hurry; the accident victim had been dead for at least forty-five minutes. As the black wagon rounded the last bend, just before the site of the horrible motorcycle accident, the driver saw a crowd gathered at the roadside. There's always a crowd. Some stop to help, others just to gawk. All wonder what happened.

In the case of this accident, no one realized that what seemed to be a tragic ending would prove to be an astonishing beginning. A perfectly ordinary day was about to change—dramatically.

Can Anybody Pray?

One moment I was in that most beautiful place called Paradise. Suddenly, I heard the words, *"I'm performing a miracle. I'm letting you live."*

Whoosh! Instantly I was back in my crumpled body. I found myself looking up at a very startled lady who had been cradling my lifeless head. Then my eyes frantically searched the faces of all those who had gathered around me, I asked as I labored to breathe, "Can *anybody* pray for me?" The crowd, mostly burly-looking men, slowly shook their heads from side to side as if in some sort of trance. "No."

As I realized what a desperate situation I was in, I repeated the question, "Can *anybody* pray for me?" Once again, as if in unison, they shook their heads. No.

Now I frantically gasped for air as my lungs quickly filled with blood. *"Somebody, please pray!"*

Then a hush fell over the crowd as one small boy pushed them all aside, kneeled in the broken glass, grease, and wreckage, slid his cap off his little head, and said, "Mister, I can."

What Are They Saying?

As the hearse arrived, the driver noticed people running around, wildly waving their arms. "What? What are they saying? He's alive? He's alive!" No, could it really be true? The attendant, heart racing, wheeled around and backed up as close as he dared. He jumped out and rushed around the vehicle to open the doors; with his hands visibly shaking, he grabbed the gurney, setting it up as quickly as possible, thinking, *Had I known he was alive I would have hurried. I thought they said this man was dead!* The driver and a bystander carefully lifted me onto the gurney as best they could. He raced off on the fifteen-minute ride to the closest hospital, a very small county hospital, which was *not* equipped to handle such a dire emergency.

There were two doctors on call. One older doctor made the comment, "There's no use to even try to save him; he's too far gone."

The younger doctor, who had just gotten back from a tour in Vietnam, said, "We're going to give it our best shot."

Blood had filled my lungs. I was crushed all over. They were not sure where to even begin, but breathing was a first priority. I watched as if it were a horror movie, as the doctor grabbed some stainless steel tubing. Realizing he was going to just jab it through my chest walls, I said, "Whoa, Doc, aren't you even going to give me anything for pain?"

"Man," he said, "you're far beyond the point of *anything* helping this pain." Then he instantly pushed the stainless steel tubes into my sides and between my ribs to drain the blood out of my lungs. The splashing, dripping, and gurgling of blood echoed in my ears as I squinted at the brightest lights I'd ever seen. The scars from those punctures still remind me of that horrific day.

Meanwhile, the waiting room was filling to overflowing and spilling over into the parking lot. People were unashamedly praying, crying out to God for mercy. Many were on their knees in the waiting room, down the halls, in the parking lot, on the lawn, and sitting on the curbs. Tears streamed down the faces of strong men, women, and children who were interceding for me. For some people, praying was a normal thing to do; for others, it had been a while since they had called on God for any reason.

God's call on my life was causing people to think about what was really important in life. During all of this, some of the family had called my wife to tell her the bad news. They hadn't told her just how bad it really was.

They put me on life support, put me on a gurney, and covered my face with a sheet before loading me in the ambulance for the ride to the Nashville hospital. As I passed the crowd, that same lady I'd seen in my dream said, "Oh no, he can't die!" They pulled the sheet down to let her see me one last time. As my eyes met hers, I heard that voice once again say, *"I'm performing a miracle, I'm letting you live."*

Still during daylight, though late in the afternoon, they put me ever so cautiously in the ambulance. A nurse from Livingston rode with me to Baptist Hospital in Nashville. She was of great encouragement to me. "Hold on. We'll soon be there. I'm taking good care of you." She was patting my hand very softly, just so I'd know she was near. She caressed my hand for the entire two hour trip.

It seemed like a very long ride. Lights were on and the sirens in full blast all the way. That sound was enough to send terror through the very soul. I was feeling very helpless, as thoughts raced through my mind like bullets. But God in His sweet mercy kept whispering in my ear, *"I'm performing a miracle."*

They Hadn't Heard the News

At this very same hour, people were gathering at a local church to hear me preach. They had not heard the news. I had already broken two appointments at this particular church, and I had said "for sure" I'd be there that night. They were crowded into that church, spilling over to the outside. It was standing room only, as they had heard of the many miracles that had been taking place everywhere I went. They had heard the accounts of many healings, deliverances, and salvations taking place. God had transformed many lives during these services. People were hungry to hear the Word of God preached in great power.

A minister friend of mine had heard about my accident and had already been to the local hospital to be with my family and pray for me. He had previously planned to go to the service that night. He knew that the congregation probably had not heard the news yet, since it had happened late in the day, so he went on to church and shared the bad news with them. Instead of hearing me preach that night, they prayed that God would spare my life and prayed for my healing. I was later told about the very powerful, anointed, and heart-wrenching prayer service that was held on my behalf.

"The Spirit of the Lord is upon me, because he hath anointed me to preach the gospel to the poor, he hath sent me to heal the brokenhearted, to preach deliverance to the captives, and recovering of sight to the blind, to set at liberty them that are bruised." (Luke 4:18)

Meanwhile

Upon arrival at Baptist Hospital—where they had already been alerted to my anticipated arrival time—they rushed me into the OR very quickly. As the doctors were pushing me down the hall, the older doctor made a huge incision into my abdomen, all the way from the breastbone right down to the bottom of the rib cage. This was done in plain sight of visitors and my family members. Time was of the essence, and there was no time for formalities.

After working on me in the OR for quite a while, one of the doctors came out to update my family. The doctor said that there was just no way I could live. He said that my liver was like a watermelon that had been dropped on the floor and had exploded. They packed my liver in gauze and just put it back into my chest cavity.

In the meantime, Thelma and two of my children had flown from Michigan down to Baptist Hospital in Nashville. When she walked into the waiting room, she was surprised to see so many of our family and friends. There had already been many prayers spoken and tears shed for me. Many were continually on their knees, praying. Thelma had also been praying. When they told her there was no chance that I would live, she said, "We are a people of faith. Howard *will* live."

The doctor told her that I was on a respirator and later returned to say—to his amazement—that my liver was still functioning. Quite a miracle in itself!

My rib cage and spine were severely crushed. Every ligament and tendon was torn. My right kidney was so damaged, they felt sure I would lose it, but I didn't.

After hours in surgery, they brought me into a recovery room. When I woke up, I was staring at the ceiling. The only thing I could move was my right hand. The doctors and nurses were still standing around. Somehow I got the attention of a nurse, who said, "Looks like he wants to write something." Frantically I'd motion more and more. Finally they brought me a pencil and paper. At this time all I could see was the ceiling, but they put the pencil in my hand and held the paper for me. I wrote, "God is performing a miracle. He's going let me live. Tell Thelma to go buy that diamond ring that she's been wanting."

The doctors were so amazed that even with the trauma I'd been through, I could even think, much less write. *No* brain damage, even after being dead for forty-five minutes. What a divine miracle!

Another tug at my heart.

Angels

While I was in ICU, angels began to visit me; however, at the time, I didn't realize they were angels. They sang the most beautiful songs I have ever heard. Each time they sang or were there in my room, there was a very soft glow that surrounded them, emitting wonderful peace and tranquility. I kept asking, "Who are the gospel singers? What radio station are you playing? Can't you hear them singing?" I could hear them even with people in the room, but nobody else could. They were all so sure the medication was causing me to hallucinate.

One night, a nurse who had been sitting with me woke me up. "Mr. Dailey, Mr. Dailey! Are you a preacher? I've never heard such dynamic preaching. I was afraid you'd have a heart attack!" I had evidently been doing some very powerful preaching in my sleep.

After several days of people just filing past me in ICU, I got really discouraged. I was giving up. Just didn't seem to be getting any better. I thought I wasn't going to make it.

When my son Bruce came in, I took hold of his hand and said, "Son, I'm not going to make it. You are going to have to take care of Mom, your sister, and your brother."

Wiping away the tears, Bruce said, "Dad, if you're not going to make it, I don't ever want to hear anything else about faith. You have believed faith, preached faith, and now you tell me you're not going to make it. Something is wrong with this picture."

That grabbed hold deep in my spirit. "Son, I *am* going to make it. I am going to make it!" This gave me courage to keep on trying.

Sent Home

After I had received many weeks of care in the hospital and was still facing a spinal fusion surgery, my insurance was maxed out. The doctors walked into my room and made the announcement. "We've done all that we can do. Your insurance has paid all they'll pay. We're now sending you home."

Ironic, isn't it? They run test after test, treatment after treatment, but when the money runs out, they push you out. Just too bad. You're on your own.

Now What?

My family managed to get me home. I had a hospital bed, even in my own house; they put it in the corner of the living room. Now we all had two new sets of problems to cope with. I couldn't help myself, but life goes on anyway. The business of a household continued, with three rambunctious kids running in and out, and I was wondering now how the bills were going to be paid. *What's next?*

Our friends and neighbors were the best, always checking in on us, bringing food, fresh garden stuff, visiting, and praying. They helped us any way they could.

After one week at home, something went terribly wrong. Even though we knew we would have to pay out of pocket for any further treatment, I was taken to Livingston Hospital for more tests. They consulted with Nashville Hospital and decided that I'd surely not make it this time. They told Thelma that I would go off into a deep sleep, then into a coma, and just go on out peacefully.

The doctors pushed me into a room to die. They kept the room very dark and quiet, as the least bit of light or noise really put my already raw nerves on edge. I was in such excruciating pain. Absolutely *nothing* would stop the pain, a pain that literally can't be described. The intensity, the sharp stabbing pain, the horror of it all was overwhelming to me.

There I lay, just waiting to die, seemingly forgotten by everyone. I was too tired to think; too tired to pray. *God, have you forgotten about me too?*

A Mighty Warrior

Across town in a simple frame home lived an elderly couple of very modest means.

Nina Hammock, a dear saint of God, was always faithful to the ministry that God had given her. Many, many times she could be found in her attic, which was lit only by a bare light bulb hanging from the ceiling on an old, frayed electrical wire. She would kneel in prayer in front of a very old handmade trunk, elbows resting on the edge, head bowed, and weathered hands folded over a tear-stained family Bible. There were well-worn hollows in the bare plank floor from bended knees and the many hours that she spent laboring in prayer.

She was so familiar with the voice of God that he only had to speak once. Ever so slowly, she pushed her way upright and slipped on her scruffy shoes. Down the short flight of creaky wooden stairs and out the door she went. There was no need to take time to tell her husband; he already knew. She was on a mission sent by God.

Having never owned a car, she thought nothing of walking the several blocks to the hospital. She hardly felt the pain of her arthritic knees.

Although we didn't know each other, she knew exactly where to go. My face had flashed before her. She knew which room to go into. "No Visitors Allowed" meant nothing to her, as she gently pushed open the door. Her eyes adjusted to the dark room. Nurses marched in right behind her. "Lady, you can't go in there."

She said, "I came to pray," and pray she did. Some of her words were understood by earthly ears and some were meant for heavenly ears only. She left me with one verse:

**"I shall not die, but live, and declare the works of the Lord."
(Psalm 118:17)**

When she had done what God told her to do, she said, "God bless you." She turned around, walked out, and pulled the door behind her.

They Thought I'd Died

Immediately I fell into a deep sleep. Thelma thought I had died, and she rushed to the nurses' station. The doctor was called in. After checking me over, he announced that I was in the most peaceful sleep he had ever seen. "Let him sleep, but call me as soon as he wakes up."

They said I slept soundly for twenty-two hours. The floor was a flurry, trying to locate the doctor when I woke up. He rushed into my room as quickly as he could.

"So, how are you feeling today?" the doctor asked.

"I feel great, but I'm starving to death!" was my reply.

"But you can't eat in your condition."

"Just get me some food, Doc, and I'll show you."

As it was close to lunchtime, he sent down for a tray of food. They brought in fried chicken, mashed potatoes, green peas, and a roll. Food never tasted so good! It's still one of my favorite meals. I promptly ate every bite and announced, "That sure was good, but I'm still starving." So, being a good doctor, he sent for a second tray, not taking his eyes off me as I consumed yet the second tray of food.

Flabbergasted would be a good way to describe the doctor that particular day. Since I seemed to have recovered from yet another near-death experience, they decided to observe me overnight. The next day, because I was still feeling fine, they sent me home.

Officially written in my hospital records were the following words: "At near death an unknown elderly lady prayed for Howard. He recovered. We're sending him home."

Once again I was brought back from the brink of death, held only by God's breath.

What a tug on a young man's heart!

Train it Wasn't

During one particularity hot sultry summer day during my recovery, I sat by the window in the living room for a short while. I was at least able to look out the window and hear, and sometimes see, the children playing. I overheard them saying that a train was coming. They ran in to tell me about the unusual sound. I said, "That's no train. That's a tornado coming!"

They helped me get to the back door just as we spotted the vicious black funnel cloud quickly gathering strength. The monster cloud was snatching any- and everything in its path. The swirling debris was flying around and around, coming directly toward us. With no safe place to go and no time to get there, even if we had a shelter, I instantly stretched out my arm, held up my hand toward the monstrous storm, and said, "In the name of Jesus, I rebuke you." It turned and went completely around us. A wonderful calm then settled around us.

What a *mighty* God we serve! Praise God! The wind and the waves still obey His spoken word.

"And he arose, and rebuked the wind, and said unto the sea, Peace, be still. And the wind ceased and there was a great calm." (Mark 4:39)

Six Million-Dollar Man

We had spent all our savings by this time, and we had to sell the business. Just managing the day-to-day living expenses with no job and three children in school was a very challenging task in itself. Some days there was absolutely nothing in the house to eat. Just when we were wondering what to do next, God would show up. Sometimes a twenty-dollar bill would just "appear" in my housecoat pocket where absolutely nothing had been earlier. In the painful condition I was in, my faithful old housecoat was about the only thing I was comfortable wearing; even then, I wouldn't say it was exactly "comfortable." Many times there would be a knock on the front door, and we would open it to find a thoughtful neighbor had prepared a delicious meal for us. God was *always* faithful. Our needs were met every time.

Because of the sheer pain I was still having, about once a week, somebody would have to take me to the hospital for a "knockout" shot of medication. No matter what was done or what I took, nothing seemed to ease to intense pain that I endured day after day.

Twenty-two months after the accident, a team of doctors at Vanderbilt did yet another study on my spine. They decided that where the spine had been crushed so badly, just the slightest movement at any given moment could sever the spinal cord. It was then they decided that with my permission, they should go in and do a spinal fusion. Even this surgery could cause permanent paralysis or even death. The surgery was a *very* high risk, but there didn't seem to be much choice. I was told to think about it for a few days.

I stood on this Scripture:

"I shall not die, but live, and declare the works of the Lord."
(Psalm 118:17)

After I had been in Vanderbilt Hospital for three weeks, the doctors asked for my decision on whether to do this surgery or not. I said, "Yes, I want it done. I'll be the next Six Million-Dollar Man! But I'd be faster and better, though!"

They took me down to surgery. I'd always heard they would ask you if you knew where you were before they would let you go back to your room. So, after several hours of delicate surgery, they wheeled me into the recovery room. They asked me the famous question. "Mr. Dailey, do you know where you are?" My response was, "I'm in the recovery room."

Later, they asked me the same dumb question yet again. I again said, "I'm in the recovery room."

"Okay," they said, "he's ready to go his room."

So, as they were wheeling me down the hall, I got hold of the bed rails, raised myself up (a big no-no, since I was not supposed to move at all) and announced, "Ladies and gentlemen, you're looking at the new Six Million-Dollar Man." I lay down and didn't wake back up for another two hours. They then realized they had taken me out of the recovery room way too soon!

I was in the hospital for several more weeks, even though I did not have insurance. I paid some out of pocket, and eventually the hospital wrote most of it off.

Yet another time God supplied our needs.

Body Cast Blues

It was quite a while after the spinal fusion before they could even put a body cast on me. With hopes of getting better, I was anxious to have this procedure done. Maybe things would soon improve. Normal? I didn't know what that meant anymore, but at least hopes of improvement were in sight. I thought it was worth the risk. After getting the body cast put on, I still had to sleep in the hospital bed in the living room when I was allowed to return home. I began to realize then, sadly, that there was a very long recovery period. I continued to be dependent on others for every single detail of life. I could not even get up and down without help. I felt like I was lying on concrete.

The days turned into weeks; weeks turned into months. The body cast made me feel like bugs were crawling in there. The oppressive summer heat can get to a person real quick. Pain was my ever-constant companion.

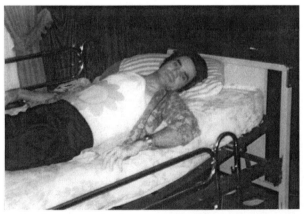

Howard at home in a body cast after the motorcycle accident.

Hours ticked by very slowly as I recovered. Even the tick-tock of the clock grated on my nerves. The small, insignificant things irritated me: the fly I couldn't swat; the wrinkles in the bed sheets; my toenails that I couldn't even cut. I was feeling totally useless. Was this ever going to be different? Would this ever end?

The kids were running in and out the house, banging the screen doors. Intense itching, pain, and sweltering heat all got to me. I had way too much time to think. *How am I going to feed my family, pay the ongoing bills and utilities?* The kids were outgrowing their clothes faster than a jackrabbit could run. *What are we going to do?*

I tried to block out the thoughts that crowded my mind. I turned my face to the wall. A tear slid down my face. Through my tear I spotted a bug crawling up the wall. *I can't even mash that stupid bug!*

Many days I'd wonder if I had heard God's voice at all. Was He *really* performing a miracle and letting me live? Is this what you call living?

Questions … questions. No answers. Sometimes we listen to the voice of the enemy. Why am I still in such bad shape? Am I being punished? I must have missed something. Had God spoken and I not heard his answer? Has He changed his mind? What? What?!

Despair would creep in and cling to my bones like the heavy Tennessee humidity hanging in the air.

Some days I became very despondent. I just did not want to go on living like this any longer. I prayed, "Lord, heal me or take me on home."

Then I would catch myself. I knew better. I would encourage myself in the Lord, just as David in the Bible had to do. I realized that my entire life had been a test of faith and I am an "ongoing miracle."

"And David was greatly distressed … but David encouraged himself in the Lord his God." (I Samuel 30:6)

Satan is a liar. This is *very* important to remember. He will tell you God's had enough of you. Satan will tell you that this time, God will not come through for you.

God would send people to come by and pray for us. Many times we were lifted from despair by the prayers of God's saints.

I learned how very important it is to do anything you can do to help and encourage people, any way you are able—whether it is a phone call, a bowl of beans and cornbread, a hug, or a prayer. It may seem small to you, but take the time to do it anyway. You will never know how much even what we might call "little things" might help someone at a very critical moment in their lives. We are God's hands on Earth. I shudder to think where I would be today if it were not for God's faithful people.

Yes, I may walk through the valley of the shadow of death. I may be in darkness. I may be where the sun doesn't shine all the time, but in spite of the shadows, I am going through! Sometimes God *makes* us lie down in the green pastures, and he leads us beside the still waters.

God said, as you walk *through* the valley of the shadow of death; He never said to *camp* in the valley. And yes, I'm walking through this valley. God is still preparing a table in the presence of my enemies. That means *right* now, not in the "sweet by and by."

"The Lord is my shepherd, I shall not want.

He maketh me to lie down in green pastures. He leadeth me beside the still waters.

He restoreth my soul: He leadeth me in the paths of righteousness for His name's sake.

Yea, though I walk through the valley of the shadow of death, I will fear no evil: for Thou art with me, Thy rod and Thy staff they comfort me.

Thou preparest a table before me in the presence of mine enemies, Thou anointest my head with oil, my cup runneth over.

Surely goodness and mercy shall follow me all the days of my life, and I will dwell in the house of the Lord forever."

(Psalm 23:1–6)

God is still on the throne, and He is still faithful!

To encourage oneself takes courage. I like to be an encourager. When I see people down, I want to pick them up, to do my best to help them. I know what despair feels like, and I know what it feels like to be on top of the world. I know what it is like to be on the bottom.

God has never let me down!

"Jesus Christ is the same yesterday, today, and forever." (Hebrews 13:8)

Itching to Preach

Even though I was in a body cast, very uncomfortable and constantly itching, I still had the call to preach. It was quite an event to get me up and out of the house. I still couldn't wear many clothes, so my ever-faithful housecoat would have to do. *For real?* Yes, I even preached in my housecoat! Standing on my feet for any length of time was painful, but I was very determined to get going. After all, God had spared my life. When God gives me a message to preach, I *have* to get it out!

They say nothing stops the mailman. He goes in the rain, sleet, or snow. Well, I've preached in a body cast, a housecoat, and as you'll soon see, even somebody else's suit!

During this time, I required a lot of help even getting up to preach, and I could not stand on my feet for long at any one time. Nobody had to worry about me being a long-winded preacher.

The doctors had cautioned me about falling. I was warned to be extremely careful, because if I fell, I might never recover. As I finished my sermon, I carefully made my way to the edge of the stage. *Ker-plunk.* Down I went. Gasps went up. I'm sure prayers went up simultaneously. But God was faithful, as all was well.

Off with the Old!

After nine long months of being confined to that body cast, the day finally arrived to have it taken off. I was more than ready!

Some days it felt like I was sleeping on the floor—just very uncomfortable. It felt like I was confined to a cage. Claustrophobia could have easily set in.

Still, they had thought I would be in it much longer than I was. God healed me faster than normal.

Since the doctors thought I would never walk again, I was dubbed "the walking miracle." After getting to the hospital and into the waiting room, I was finally taken back to the exam room. They then laid me on the table. They first X-rayed me and were excited that the fusion had taken so well. After setting the tray up with the needed equipment, they went to work on me.

The whirring sounds that the saw made were both unnerving and exciting. As the cast came off, the fresh air touching my skin at first felt *so* good; then it felt as if part of me was missing. It was a very strange feeling. Catching that first glimpse of my skin made me literally gasp. It was very scaly and gray, and it looked and smelled rotten. I thought I'd never look "right" again. My skin was very sensitive for quite a while after that. Thankfully, this too passed. The best feeling, though, was to get home and get into the shower. Water, oh wonderful water, gently cascading down my body. It felt so wonderful! I almost felt normal.

The body cast was history! Free at last, or was I?

A week later, I was to be fitted with a body brace, but I did have much more freedom to move around. It would take time for my muscles to work correctly and to get stronger.

I was still in so much pain and still having to be taken to the hospital at least once a week for the knockout shots. Was I addicted to pain medication? No, I *had* to have it just to survive!

Later on, I realized that I really was addicted to the pain medication. I had been in very critical shape when I had the accident. Nobody really expected me to live, so they gave me the maximum amount of painkiller that they could possibly give me. Only, when I did survive, I was already addicted to the medication. I would have to address this problem at a later time.

Totally Broke

During my recuperation, I was getting around better but unable to go back to work. Our bills were way past due, and the cupboards were literally bare.

God always provided for our needs, many times at seemingly the very last minute. At times I wondered if God knew what time it was or just how late it was getting to be. Or maybe this time, was He going to let me down?

Early one Saturday morning, God showed me a vision. In a flash, I saw "the picture." God told me to go to a church in Harlan, Kentucky, and deliver two messages. This was a church I'd never been to, and I did not know the pastor.

We rushed around and got ready to go. Beulah lived close to this church, so we headed her way. We had barely enough gas in the car to get us there and just enough money to get across the Daniel Boone Toll Road. After that, I would be totally broke, doing what God showed me to do and trusting Him for the rest.

I hadn't even called Beulah to tell her that we were coming. She was cooking supper when we arrived. She's one of the South's finest cooks, so it is always a special treat to eat with her.

After supper, she said that if we felt like it, we could go to a benefit singing in Harlan, Kentucky. I said, "I feel like it. Let's go!"

So off we went. The service was starting just as we got there. We quietly slipped in and sat near the back. I whispered to my wife, "This is the very same church that I saw in my vision!"

The pastor, who was sitting on the platform, looked straight at me. He got up and came back to us and said, "God said that you have a message for this church tonight."

"I sure do," was my reply.

He then told me that the singing was supposed to be a benefit for the building fund but that he would have them do a few songs and let me preach.

The singers sang some wonderful old hymns, and then the church took up the offering. I preached the message that God had given me, and then I gave an altar call. Twenty-seven people were saved.

I turned the service back to the pastor. He spoke before the congregation, and said that normally he would have a meeting with the decons to do what he was planning, but he felt that the visiting minister (me) was in great financial need. He then presented me with that nights collection. Awestruck, I thanked them, and stuck the envelope of money inside my coat pocket.

Standing by the back door as the congregation leaves has always been my custom, as I like to speak to the people. They kept on giving me more money. As they did, I put the money in my left pocket. One elderly man, dressed in rumpled bib overalls, pressed a bill in my hand, and for some reason I remember putting that money in my right pocket.

It had been a good service, and I was tired but felt good knowing I had delivered the message that God had showed me early that morning.

As we started on our way back to my sister's house, I remembered that my gas tank was flat on empty. I was sure hoping something was still open this late. Sure enough, one little country market was still open. I reached in my right pocket and pulled out the bill that the old man had given me. It was a crisp new one hundred-dollar bill! I was then told that the old man with the bibbed overalls owned that very market, plus half the county. I've always heard that one should never judge a book by its cover!

But wait, there's even more.

Dust Flying

Despite the fact that it was Sunday, I decided to sleep in, being very tired and needing to get my strength back. We leisurely got up to another bountiful home-cooked meal prepared by my sister. After eating, we went out to sit in the rocking chairs on the front porch.

Looking off into the distance, we saw an old car come barreling down the holler. Dust was a-flying behind it from off the dry gravel road. The driver jumped out and ran to the house, saying, "Uncle Howard, where were you? The church was packed out! Everybody thought that you were going to preach again this morning!"

We went back to the church that night to deliver the second message that God gave me. Twenty-seven more people were saved at this service also.

On Monday morning, we got up and went back home to Tennessee. When we got home, we sat at the kitchen table and for the first time opened the offering envelope. There was seventeen hundred dollars inside! This was *in addition* to all the cash that was handed to me at the door as people left. It was more than enough money to catch up our bills and buy groceries for my family.

"But God shall supply all your needs according to his riches in glory by Christ Jesus." (Philippians 4:19)

Wrong Number

The jarring ring of the telephone startled me from a rare and much-needed deep sleep. By the aggravated voice, the obviously very drunken man had certainly not entertained the thought of talking to a preacher. But God had a different plan.

Now, since I was awake, I might as well talk to him. He was trying to reach an acquaintance who would take him back to the same nightclub he had been to earlier in the evening. He was quite upset that I had the audacity to even answer the phone. After all, I wasn't the friend he was trying to reach. Anyway, his reasoning, such as it was, seemed to make perfect sense to him.

I realized he was a very troubled and lonely soul who just needed somebody to talk to. He needed a friend, and he needed to sober up. Over the next two hours, I continued making conversation with him until he calmed down and sobered up somewhat. I told him that I was a preacher. I even told him where I lived and gave him my phone number.

It was one of the coldest nights of that winter, and he told me how hard it was just to keep warm in his old shack. He had to keep throwing wood on the fire, and the stovepipe was already glowing red hot.

I shared the gospel of Jesus with him. After I explained how he needed to repent of his sins, he then asked Jesus to come into his life and save him. We had a glorious time on the phone.

I made sure he remembered my name and phone number and told him to feel free to call me back anytime. After repeating the information I had given him, he hung up, only to call me back a couple hours later. He was still excited about his wonderful experience and thanked me again.

Reading the newspaper only a few days later, I was stunned. The headline read, "House Fire Claims Victim." It turned out to be the very same man who had called me by mistake, or so it had seemed at the time.

My heart fell. But God reminded me, "Yes, but because of your obedience, one more soul was rescued for My kingdom."

Is Hell Real?

While pastoring my first church (before the accident), I had started a program broadcasting live once a week from the radio station. It touched the hearts of many people, reaching people who might find it difficult to come into a church that they were unfamiliar with. The shut-ins really enjoyed it. It gave encouragement to many people. Now, after my accident, I felt very strongly that this was something I could do again. I would tape the sermons and have someone hand deliver them to the station. I always stated my address and phone number if anybody felt the need to call me.

The message that I had taped that day had been about the rich man and Lazarus, found in Luke 16. The beggar had died and was carried by the angels into Abraham's bosom. The rich man died and was buried. He lifted up his eyes from hell.

One particular Sunday, the program had just gone off the air, and I was sitting on the front porch, enjoying the birds singing and watching the squirrels playing with each other. Two ladies drove up in our circular driveway. They rolled their windows down and asked me if I was the same Preacher Dailey they had been listening to on their radio. They had some questions about the message they had just heard. They wanted to know if there really was a hell. And were the flames real?

After I answered yes to their questions, they were both ready to give their hearts to God. They were excited about their newfound relationship with the Lord. It always makes my day to know I have helped someone along the way.

Soft as Whispers

A turning point in my life was taking place, and I hadn't even realized it. Often I'd find myself wondering why in the world my life was the "same old, same old" every day. True, I was much better since the accident, but was this it? Was this the best I was ever going to be? Had I been brought back to life just for *this?* Yes, I was making a difference in the lives of some people. I still had the radio ministry and enjoyed occasionally getting to preach. Sometimes I'd go to the hospital and pray for people. My family loved me, and I sure loved them. I had many friends, but there was this growing longing in my heart to do more of what God had called me to do. I also often wondered if I would ever get to enjoy the wonders of life that I used to take for granted. There had to be more to life than just existing from day to day.

Deep in my spirit, I began to hear words forming, beginning as soft as whispers and as gentle as early morning dewdrops dropping from a single rose petal. Eventually they became even louder than rolling thunder. These thoughts were piercing the dark clouds of my soul as surely as quick flashes of lightning bolts dance across a blackened sky. Again and again I kept hearing the words "I *shall* live and not die and declare the works of the Lord!"

I *knew* in that moment a turning point was taking place in my life!

I prayed that God would give me wisdom and *show* me the way of change, a better way. I knew that God was my "Way Maker" and that He is a God of second chances, even when we aren't deserving of them. I *knew* that he heard that prayer!

A Welcome Prophecy

We were invited by some friends to go to a gospel singing; that is, if I felt up to sitting that long. We decided to go. It would be a welcome change for us.

We enjoyed listening to several wonderful groups. Another group had been singing for a while, when abruptly they stopped in the middle of a song. As long as I live, I'll never forget the song they sang: "Put Your Hand to the Gospel Plow and Hold On." One of the singers pointed her finger straight at Thelma and said that God was speaking to her. "Just like Joseph in the Bible, your seventh year is almost over. There's a new beginning starting for your family."

Sure enough, there was a very big and might I say welcome change starting to take place. God was answering my prayer for that change. He's still a "Way Maker" even today!

Reflexology

A what? You want me to go where? Why, I'd never in all my life heard anything about reflexology. What was this friend thinking?

The accident had left my spine and my rib cage crushed. My liver had exploded, and the ligaments in my legs were badly torn.

Experts in the medical field didn't think I would live or ever walk again. They certainly *never* thought I would ever work again. I was without an income for seven years. They had me in and out of the hospital many times. About once a week, somebody would have to take me to the hospital for shots of morphine.

A minister friend had been telling me about a reflexologist by the name of Dr. Roy Maddux. He even said that if I would just go, he'd pay for the session and all the herbs and vitamins that the doctor might suggest.

After months of his insisting, I gave in and decided to give this reflexology a try, not even knowing what this meant. This decision proved to be one of those life-changing moments of a lifetime!

Absolutely Amazed

Dr. Maddux—most folks just referred to him as "Doc"—told me to have a seat. He told me to pull off my shoes and socks. He sat in front of me with my feet in his hands and went to work rubbing, massaging, and observing my feet. I hadn't filled out any paperwork telling him anything about my situation. I sat there totally in awe at what he told me within fifteen minutes of just rubbing my feet!

Doc told me that my spine was torn up. My liver was very toxic. He named every single ailment that I had! He also told me that the medication that I was taking was killing me. He suggested that I should detoxify my body and take several particular herbs and vitamins. I was very excited about even the possibility of getting better! I went straight home and poured all my pills down the commode. That was one of the best decisions I had ever made. My addiction to the pain medication was just erased. What a God we serve! I was *so* ready to get better, and God was using this method for my healing. Within one week of starting the sessions, I started seeing a profound difference. I was truly amazed!

It seems strange that something so simple that has been around for thousands of years and is so readily available, is known by very few people.

Within a very short time of starting the reflexology sessions and taking the supplements that Doc Maddux recommended, I started noticing that I felt much better. I felt stronger with each passing day, and I was finally seeing a light at the end of the long, dark tunnel.

Do What?

At 4:00 AM one Monday, I was awakened out of a deep sleep by an audible voice. *"Howard, go see Doc Maddux."*

I got up out of bed and flipped the light on. There was nobody there. I lay back down.

Again I heard, *"Howard, go see Doc Maddux."* Same thing—I got up, flipped the light on. Once again, nobody was there. I lay back down.

Then, a third time, I heard an audible voice say, *"Howard, go see Doc Maddux. I want you to become a reflexologist."*

"Lord, is that you speaking to me?"

I heard the audible voice of God say *"Yes."* One just can't get much more distinct than that.

This time I got up out of bed, took a shower, and put a suit on.

My wife got up, took one look, and said, "What in the world are you doing up so early, and why do you have a suit on?"

"I'm going to go see Doc Maddux and become a reflexologist," I answered.

Cocking one eyebrow and looking at me sideways, she replied, *"Sure you are."*

I couldn't wait for the store to open up. When I got there, several people were already lined up to see him.

Doc said, "What are you doing here? You're not supposed to be back for another week."

"I need to talk to you," I managed to respond.

"Okay, you'll have to wait till I get caught up," Doc replied.

Soon he took me into a small, cluttered office. "Okay, son, what's on your mind?"

I told him that I wanted to become a reflexologist and asked how to go about it. He gave me a phone number and told me to call some people in Florida. He said I could use his phone. I did as I was told but was crestfallen when they told me how much money it would cost. There just seemed to be no way, since we were totally broke. When I told Doc the bad news, he told me to hang around till lunchtime. He'd buy my lunch, and we could continue our conversation.

Over lunch, I nervously shared with him just how broke I was, with the bills and having no job, and I shared with him about the audible voice of God that woke me up that morning, telling me to become a reflexologist.

Doc said, "Man, are you telling me the truth?"

Of course I was. I certainly wouldn't make up something as dramatic as that! I had never even entertained the thought of doing so.

I did tell him that I'd never been so intrigued with anything in my entire life: how one could tell so much about somebody just by the nerve endings in their feet. I learned that Doc was at retirement age and had always wanted somebody to take over his practice.

"Doc, I will be glad to learn this. I'll do everything I can to learn as quickly as possible."

He could tell that I was really sincere about this undertaking. He then told me that he would train me, teach me about the herbs and vitamins, and send me to seminars. What a gift! Wow!

He asked me when I could start. I told him immediately. He wanted to know how many days a week I could train. I told him every day. He told me to come in the very next morning to start. I trained under Doc Maddux for a total of four years and bought the store from him after two years. Is God a good God or what?

Although many people call me "the foot doctor," I'm not an MD but an RCR, which means a registered certified reflexologist.

My practice of reflexology is one that is called by God: a ministry of God's own choosing. I practice in a health-food store that I own. As of the writing of this book, I have been in business for twenty-six years. It is always rewarding to know that I have helped someone and made such a vast difference in the lives of so many people. I am always amazed at the many people God sends from far and near and from all walks of life. Some people come to me as a last resort. Many are already accustomed to taking supplements and using alternative healing. Some people say that God told them to stop in, and some say that they don't even know why they came. But I always know that God sent them to my store for a very special reason. I am blessed beyond measure as people seek out my help. It is an honor and a privilege. I will continue this ministry as long as God wants me to do so.

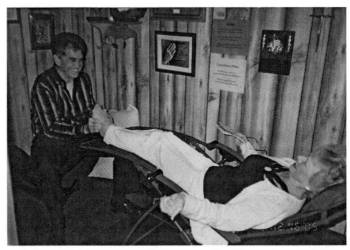

Howard and Janice Gowan during a reflexology session. Photo by Barbara Pannell

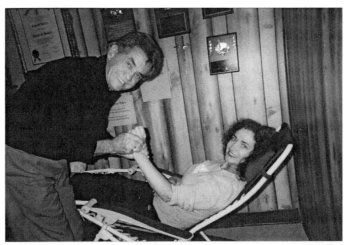

Howard and Anita Chadwell enjoying a reflexology session. Photo by Barbara Pannell

God gave me a unique dual calling. One is reflexology, as I work on the *soles* of people's feet, helping them to have better health. This is an extension of the calling that God also gave me in working for their *souls,* or their eternal destiny.

Reflexology brought many changes. Once again, I was finally able to work, and once again I felt the call to pastor a church. Together, Buddy Reed, a pastor friend, and I founded a new community church which we called Swallow's Chapel. It was a small country church, but many miracles took place during this time.

A Very Special Birthday Gift

A special client, Burnice Wesbrooks, a longtime Church of Christ minister, wrote a poem and gave it to me for my birthday in 2003. It means so much to me and I want to share that poem. It is self-explanatory and very touching. I treasure all the years of our friendship.

"The Gentle Touch of Howard's Hands"

In 1999 I rode a misery train
After cancer surgery in March
My daily burden was awful pain.
With swollen ankles I could hardly walk:
Behind the scenes I used a cane.
My back was bent, my energy gone;
I felt my health was down the drain.
Then a thoughtful niece of mine
Came and whispered in my ear,
"I think I know what you should do.
Seek a good herbalist and reflexologist,
See what he can do for you!"
I found a man named Howard Dailey
He met me with a cordial smile.
I told him my name and said, "I'm in pain."
He replied, "I'll make your visit worthwhile.
Go sit in that reclining chair
And we'll consider your needs.
Let's look for flowers among hurting thorns;

Let's produce good fruit and get rid of weeds!"
He held my feet in his gentle hands
And he began to massage my soles.
Like water from a spout the pain flowed out;
He was rubbing away those painful woes.
He methodically massaged my feet
And identified my aches and pain.
He helped bring sunshine to my life
And lessened the clouds and rain.
Five days after my first treatment
I noticed a decrease of body pain.
The swelling left my ankles
And I laid aside my walking cane.
I take the herbs like he suggests
And every now and then
I sit in that reclining chair
And commit my feet to his gentle hands.
You may be on a misery train
Like I rode in nineteen ninety-nine.
Your daily burden may be awful pain
From head to toe and in the spine.
You may be wondering how you'll face
The hours ahead each day and night.
You may be yearning, seeking, praying
That relief from pain will come in sight.
Commit your soul in daily life
To Jesus Christ, our Lord and Friend,
And then entrust the soles of your feet
To the gentle touch of Howard's hands.

—written by Burnice Wesbrooks and given to Howard Dailey for his birthday December 12, 2003. Used by permission

Burnice Wesbrooks (writer of the poem) and Howard. Photo by
Barbara Pannell

Miracles and More

On one particular Sunday morning while I was pastoring a small country church, I had just gotten started with the sermon when the doors to the sanctuary suddenly burst open. Some children ran down the center aisle, stopped, and spoke with my associate pastor. He stood up and said, "I gotta leave. My wife just died!"

I handed the microphone to a deacon and asked him to take over. I was right behind them. Their house was a few miles from the church. When I got there, the children and grandchildren were wringing their hands and screaming, "She's dead, she's dead!"

We all quickly gathered in her room. She had been dead for several minutes by now. Without even a second thought, I jumped in the bed and grabbed her up in my arms. I shouted, "In the name of Jesus, I command life to come back into this lady!"

Soon, life came back into her body. Her color came back into her face and she started talking to us. Immediately, excitement, amazement, and thankfulness filled that room to overflowing. God's wonderful presence was like a soft glow hugging everyone in that bedroom. What a service to have! How exciting can life get!

The family was running around, now screaming, "She's alive! She's alive! Mom's alive!"

This lady lived another three years before going home to be with the Lord. It is too late to tell me—or any of the people in that room—that miracles are not for today. I have seen the dead raised on several occasions. God is alive and well and still in the miracle business!

On my scale, that's a big one. On God's scale, it's just everyday stuff.

Another remarkable healing took place one Sunday morning at our church. A young married lady by the name of Becky who attended our church had unfortunately previously suffered a stroke. Still being faithful, she came to church services anyway, despite having to sit in a wheelchair during worship. During the sermon, the Lord spoke to me to tell Becky that if she would just get up and walk, she would be healed. I obeyed and told her what God had just impressed in my spirit to tell her. With a halting start, Becky slowly pushed herself up and out of her wheelchair. Ever so slowly, one halting step after another, she gained strength and momentum. Healing came as she walked down the aisle. Nobody was as surprised as she! When they came back to church that night, she told the congregation that she and her husband had spent the entire afternoon walking around Walmart. She was enjoying what most of us take for granted. God is so good!

Walking on Water

While pastoring a small church, I was asked to go to the hospital to pray for an alcoholic man who was not given much chance to live.

I prayed for him, and he asked Jesus to come into his heart and save him. We invited him to come to church when he got out of the hospital, and suggested that he needed to be baptized. He did indeed come to our church and made public his confession, and he asked to be baptized.

Being a very small country church, we still baptized in the creek. That Sunday, it had rained for several days and it had been what we call a "gully washer." What was normally a slow, meandering, picturesque creek now had a swift and deep current. Nevertheless, after church we all met at Spring Creek to baptize this man.

The congregation reverently gathered around the side of the creek, quietly singing "Shall We Gather at the River," as we gingerly made our way down into the muddy, rushing water. I was holding very tightly onto a small sapling to keep from getting carried downstream in the swift current. I placed one hand on his shoulder, and the other reached to the heavens as I prayed. Then, putting one hand behind his head and the other hand over his nose, I immersed him. The dear man was so full of the Holy Spirit and excited that when he realized he was truly born again and baptized, he came up from the water shouting at the top of his lungs. He took off running downstream, all on *top* of the water. He then turned around and ran back *upstream* to where I was, still standing in the swift current. My jaw dropped open in sheer surprise. Let me repeat, he ran on *top* of that water! Nothing had prepared me for the surprise of that moment. It's one that I will never forget. The transformation of this dear soul was so profound, no one could deny there had been a vast change. What a day!

A Sunday afternoon baptizing in Spring Creek. Photo by Barbara Pannell

Another Sunday baptism in Spring Creek. Photo by Barbara Pannell

New Heart

A severe heart problem had been troubling a pastor friend of mine for quite a while. Not wanting to worry anybody, he had not shared this information with anyone other than his wife and his father. His doctor had confirmed that his heart had not been functioning correctly for at least six months

One Sunday, I had been invited to preach at his church. Many times as I'm delivering a sermon, God allows me to experience the pain of others. This was to be one of those times.

When the pain in my chest became almost unbearable, I literally had to hold on to the podium to keep from collapsing. As the pain intensified, I realized the pain that I was now feeling was not mine. I said, "There's somebody in this service that has a heart problem. God says that if you will just come forward, He is wanting to heal you."

At this time, the congregation was already standing, but nobody came forward.

As my pain was intensifying, I repeated what God had just spoken to me. The pastor was standing in the front row beside his precious wife. Head bowed, he was praying. He thought maybe this was meant for somebody else, he didn't want to step out, if it indeed was meant for someone other than him.

Then, God spoke into that pastor's spirit, *"This is the avenue that I'm using for your healing."* He stepped out and was instantly healed! My chest pain stopped as he was healed.

Next came his testimony confirming his healing. There was an exuberant celebration about this wonderful miracle that night.

At his next doctor's appointment, they confirmed that he indeed had a new heart.

God is so very good!

A Lesson in Obedience

"...Behold, to obey is better than sacrifice..." (I Samuel 15:22)

We heard about an awesome tent revival that was being held in Albany, Kentucky. We did not know the evangelist at that time, but we had heard, "You sure don't want to miss this one!" We made our plans to attend that night.

Having been told about the standing-room-only crowds, we arrived a little early to ensure we got good seats.

The excitement was already building as the sun was setting and the crisp fall air surrounded us. The anointing fell as quickly as the evangelist picked up her guitar and she and the singers began to praise and worship the Lord. Soon all the crowd was on their feet, joining in the worship.

The message was very powerful and very moving. As the invitation was given, many people quickly filled the aisles and moved toward the altar. They never seemed to notice the dirty sawdust floors that they knelt on as they prayed and asked Jesus to come into their hearts. Many manifestations of the Spirit were evident as they cried out to God and their needs were met.

After the service, Thelma and I met the evangelist for the first time. We exchanged names and phone numbers. Our spirits just seemed to connect immediately. That was to be the beginning of a wonderful friendship with Dorothy Jo Owens. She later invited me to minister with her in a tent revival in her hometown of Pigeon Forge, Tennessee. She had a stage built in a field close to her home, and she would have a tent set up and regularly hold gospel meetings there.

Sometimes God will test us with some very unusual requests just to see if we were listening to His still, quiet voice. Will we obey what would appear to our small minds to be quite strange?

The night before this particular meeting, God told me to cut twelve-inch squares of white material and bring them to the service. Surely I hadn't heard that right, so off I went without heeding the request.

During the service that night, just as God had pricked me in the Spirit and reminded me that I was *supposed* to have brought those white squares of cloth, a lady stood up and asked if she could speak. She then told us that God had earlier spoken to her to cut up a bed sheet into twelve-inch squares, which she had done, but she too thought it sorta strange and had left them in her car. As I then related to the congregation what God had told me, she ran to the car to get the cloths and began passing them out to everybody. As she did, the power of God fell on that place in a mighty way. As we waved them in surrender to God, many wonderful manifestations of the Spirit occurred.

This sweet lady who had obeyed God, Avie Lee Owens Parton, was a sister to the evangelist, Dorothy Jo Owens, and mother to Dolly Parton. We were blessed to have several of her family members attend many of our services after that.

Over the years, Dorothy Jo became one of our dearest friends, oftentimes stopping by for a visit, and many times staying a night or even a week at a time. We enjoyed deep discussions, prayer, and Bible study together. We were like family to each other, and truly we are part of "the family of God." On several occasions, she would minister in the church that I pastored. "Daddy Was an Old-Time Preacher Man" was the most-requested song at our church. It was by far the favorite.

Once a year, a singing was held in the same area where the tent meetings were held, out in the field beside Dorothy Jo's home. Many people came in their campers, as we had, and stayed a few days. Early that first morning, the wonderful aroma of country bacon, eggs, gravy, and homemade biscuits awakened me after a late night. Was it my imagination, or was I just hoping for a good breakfast? I went out to investigate. Sure enough, there was Willadeene, another one of Dolly's sisters, cooking the biggest breakfast one could imagine! Being the helpful guy I like to think I am, I asked her if I could help, but when she told me to clean the skillet that she had cooked gravy in, I began looking around, wondering how in the world was I to accomplish that task with no running water. It was then that she had a good-natured laugh on me. She taught me how to "make do" by scrunching up aluminum foil and wiping the pan out. It really worked well, and we got to enjoy her wonderful cooking.

In the fall of 2007, we were delighted to attend the beautiful afternoon wedding of Dorothy Jo to her soul mate, Bill Parton. The setting was outdoors in her beloved Smokey Mountains with a meandering creek as a backdrop for the special occasion. Her niece, Stella Parton, performed the ceremony, and Dolly Parton walked her down the rose petal-strewn grass aisle to meet her beaming groom. It was a sweet moment when Dolly "gave her away." It was a very special day and a *beautiful* wedding, one we will never forget.

Dolly Parton with (bride) Dorothy Jo, (groom) Bill Paton, and wedding party. Photo by Barbara Pannell

Then later, at the reception, Dolly sang one of her most popular songs to the bride and groom, changing just a few of the words of "I Will Always Love You" to be more appropriate for this occasion, which was a delight to everyone there.

As a bonus, Dolly was lucky enough to get her picture taken with *me* at the wedding rehearsal the previous night. (Just kidding, Dolly! It's *me* who got lucky.) Thanks, Dolly. The picture proudly hangs in my office and inspires lots of conversations.

Dolly Parton and Howard. Photo by Barbara Pannell

On a much more somber note, Dorothy Jo was "chosen" to enjoy the wonders of heaven certainly much sooner than we would have wanted. Although we still miss her on this side of eternity, I *know* she is the lucky one.

Peeking Through the Casket Flowers

Serving the Lord Can Be Dangerous! I just never thought that serving the Lord would be so hazardous. Most people never think of it that way, but it sometimes can be, and at the oddest times!

On a summer day, I was asked to hold the funeral of a ninety-eight-year-old lady. I just couldn't say no to this request, even though I barely knew her family.

The day of the funeral turned out to be one of those hot, sultry summer days that Tennessee is famous for. The viewing of the body had been held in her home, and then the funeral home was to have her body at the country church at an appointed hour. However, misjudging the time element and being further out than they anticipated, the church was packed and waiting. With no air conditioning, nerves were getting on edge. Those handheld fans were frantically doing all they could do.

As the time to start the funeral finally arrived, the family filed in and sat in the usual front rows. Unknown to me, in walked two of her sons, in shackles and chains and with two security guards. Next came a daughter in shackles and chains, with *her* security guard. Neither of the guards were armed.

Finally, they arrived with the dear departed and I started the service. Only two minutes into the service, another one of the sons who had been sitting in the front row jumped up, waving a gun, and started shouting, "I'm going to kill all of you!" He was hollering, cursing, and carrying on something awful. Then the ruckus really broke out. I fell straight to the floor behind the podium. I found *one* little peephole in all those casket flowers from which to view this commotion. As soon as the officers got control of the situation, I swallowed hard and cautiously got back up to

93

the podium. Trying hard not to let my voice quiver, I then said, "Folks, this dear lady has been through enough already." I said a brief prayer, and I do mean *brief.* I dismissed them and I was outta there!

Gun Held to My Head

Late one night, a woman called me to come to her house. There was a problem with her family, and she needed somebody to talk with them. I didn't know them very well, but they had visited our church a couple of times. I make it a practice to take another pastor or deacon with me anytime something of this nature occurs, but on this particular night, there was no one available to go with me, so I went on anyway. I had to pull up in front of the house, since there was no place to park in the driveway. When I arrived, I got out of the car to go to the door, and a man stepped out of the dark shadows. He wanted to know what I was doing there. Not knowing what his wife had told him about calling me, or if she had even told him at all, I told him I came to talk to him about the Lord. I then realized that he had a gun in his hand. His wife came out of the house about that time. The man started hollering, "I'm going to kill you all!" He pointed the gun at his wife, who was only two or three feet away. He pulled the trigger, but the gun did not go off. I realized he was stoned out of his mind on both drugs and alcohol.

His brother, hearing the commotion, came out of his house, which was next door. The woman's husband then pointed the gun at his brother and again pulled the trigger, but again it did not go off. Now, it was my turn. The man pointed the gun directly in my face and pulled the trigger. Again it did not go off.

This being a very serious situation, I started commanding, in the name of Jesus Christ, the demons that were controlling him to come out of this man. Suddenly, he came to himself and said, "What have I done? Where am I?"

I told him that he had just tried to kill his wife, his brother, and me. I then took the gun from him and put it in my pocket.

The brother—not wanting to get involved any further—went back to his house.

I stayed, talked, and prayed with them for a couple of hours. Just before going home, I asked to be excused to go to the restroom, using that as an excuse to take a look at the gun.

I pulled the gun out of my pocket and realized the safety was indeed off and had been ready to fire. *Well,* I thought to myself, *it must not really have any ammo in it.* I pulled the magazine out, and it was fully loaded with live ammo. *Well, surely it must not have any in the chamber.* Lord, this gun was fully loaded!

God then said, *"I didn't let the gun go off. You were always in my protection."*

"No weapon formed against you shall prosper..." (Isaiah 54:17)

Doberman Pinschers

Late one night, I received a call from a family, asking me to pray for a man who was very sick, and they wanted to know if I'd come over. I called another pastor, Buddy Reed, to go with me. Buddy and I worked together very closely. He was always willing to go with me to pray, so I picked him up in my old car. We drove out to their house, which was in the country.

We pulled into the driveway, and two Doberman pinschers—two of the biggest dogs I have ever seen—came running up to the front of the car. They meant business. In the headlights of the car, all we could see were teeth, huge teeth at that! And to top it off, my old car's horn didn't even work. I tried racing the motor; I thought that might scare them off, but to no avail. The people in the house were oblivious to our situation and didn't even know we were out there.

"Well," Buddy said, "now what are we going to do?"

"We're going to do what we always do: pray. Rebuke the devil that is controlling those dogs," I replied. So, in the name of Jesus, I rebuked that devil. Immediately, God shut the dogs' mouths. Those dogs just lay right down in front of the car, crossed their paws, and laid their heads down on their feet.

We got out and walked around the car, around the dogs and onto the porch, and knocked on the door. One of the family members opened the door and quickly jerked us inside. "How'd you get past those dogs?"

"We prayed and just walked past them."

One of the family members said that when we were ready to leave, they would have to put those dogs up or they would tear us to pieces. They couldn't understand how we ever got past the vicious dogs in the first place.

We talked about the Lord, prayed for the family, and stayed for a couple of hours. We forgot about the dogs.

When we went back to our car, we opened the doors, got in, and turned the car's headlights on. There were those two vicious dogs, ever so peaceful and still lying right in front of the car, just like we had left them.

"God is our refuge and strength, a very present help in trouble." (Psalm 46:1)

Did You Say Copperhead?

I was holding services in a little country church in the Tennessee hills one hot summer day. The sermon was on how we have the power of God.

I said, "We have the power to tread on serpents, scorpions, and over all the power of the enemy."

As was my usual custom, "I get down there amongst them," as Jerry Clower used to say, walking the aisles and eating that mike like an ice-cream cone. As I was walking down the aisle, near the back door, my eyes caught a glimpse of … what in the world? A snake came slithering toward me. Silently I prayed, "God, what am I to do?" All the while, I'd been preaching that we have the power to tread on all the power of the enemy. The snake came closer and closer. By this time, my heart was pounding harder and harder.

Howard preaching. Photo by Barbara Pannell

There I was, preaching that we have the power, but silently praying, "God, that's a *real* snake!"

"Son, do you really believe my Word is real?"

Okay, this was getting serious and fast!

One more time, I walked down that aisle with that power to tread upon serpents and all the power of the enemy, and just as I said, "We have the power," with one swift blow, the heel of my cowboy boot came smashing down on its head. Tossing the dead snake aside, I kept right on preaching.

There was only one wide-eyed lady who saw what happened. She was wise enough not to disrupt God's victory over that devil.

Only as I picked it up on a stick after services and tossed that old serpent out in victory did anybody even realize what had just taken place.

That very same day, in the same area, there were two other churches that had snakes visiting their services also. Their services were dismissed—shall we say, early!

"Behold, I give unto you power to tread on serpents and scorpions, and over all the power of the enemy; and nothing shall by any means hurt you." (Luke 10:19)

Please God, Not on Mother's Day

The last breath drawn. The nurse clasped her hands together and let out a long, rueful sigh. Too bad the family, who had waited all this time, had not been in the room for her departure. Unfortunately, not knowing the patient's time remaining on Earth was so short, the nurse had asked them to step outside for a few minutes while she performed her duties. The patient had seemed like such a pleasant lady. The nurse finished this last task at hand by adjusting the sheets before letting the family return for one last visit with their mother.

At best, even when the family is expecting death, it's still a hard thing to tell them. The seasoned nurse drew a deep breath and stepped outside the door where they were anxiously waiting. Having told them the sad but expected news, she stepped aside as they filed into the room. As they gathered around the bed, the nurse stood at the back of the room. Soft sobs of sorrow arose; tears flowed freely as they reluctantly said their good-byes.

I was standing to the left side of mom's hospital bed. I dropped my head, eyes still moist from the raw emotions that I'd been experiencing. I rested my arm on the cold metal bedrail and reached for her little wrinkled hand one last time. Looking at her sweet face once more, I glanced up just as the sun came streaming over the edge of the parking lot. I had just noticed that the dogwood trees were in full bloom and realized it was the dawning of a new day. The past few days had been very stressful ones. Too much coffee, not enough sleep, pacing the hospital halls, and thumbing through way too many well-worn magazines.

Was it a prayer? I know not, but I said, "God, if I could have just one more request, it would be that Mom had not died on Mother's Day."

Suddenly, her eyelids blinked open. "Son, I'm here."

That sweet voice! Was I hearing things? Startled gasps of joy and excitement rose in that room. Everybody was hugging first Mom, then each other. What a miracle.

Stunned, the nurse even began to question her own ability to determine life and death. Still, she was very happy for the family and glad the patient was alive. It was more than enough to cause a buzz in the break room that day.

I visited with Mom for quite a while, but not wanting to wear her out, I told her I'd go on out into the waiting room awhile. Some others in the family had been waiting to come in. They said they would be there awhile, so I could go home, shower, and put on fresh clothes. I then went back to the hospital to sit with Mom for the remainder of the day and into the wee hours of the night. I went home just before daybreak.

I got home just as the first rays of the morning sun peeked over the trees. Tired to the bone, I heard the phone ringing as I opened the front door. The voice on the other end said, "Howard, Mom just went on home to be with the Lord. We're here waiting for the undertaker."

My wife and I jumped in the car and raced back to the hospital.

The same nurse was there once again, this time making sure of the death. She told us we could go in and see her.

Once again, taking her frail hand in mine, I said, "God, if you could grant me one more prayer, I would have like to have been here to tell Momma good-bye."

Once again, I heard that familiar sweet voice. "Son, I'm here."

"I just wanted to tell you bye. It's okay, you can go on home now."

This time, Mom closed her eyes for the last time, having a sweet peace about her. She went home to be with her Lord and Savior.

If the Suit Fits

There's an old saying that goes, "If the shoe fits, wear it."

Well, I'm not so sure that applies here, but in country song style, it goes something like this.

There was a big crusade being held in the area where I live. Lots of home folks, kinfolks, church folks, and friends would be there to hear me preach. My nephew Steve Dailey and his wife Darlene, who pastor a big church in Indianapolis, Indiana, had come down to minister in music for this special occasion. So, wanting to help set up the stage, speakers, and just generally get everything ready for the service, I left home wearing my jeans. Earlier in the day, my wife had picked my suit up from the local dry cleaners. Wanting to look spiffy like we preachers tend to do, I was very careful not to wrinkle it.

We could hear the roar of the crowd already gathering. I made my way back to the dressing room and slipped on the nicely starched shirt and tie. Slipping on the trousers, I thought, *My, am I losing weight? Naw ... but what's going on here?* I quickly realized that the cleaners had made a *terrible* mistake. They had switched my suit. This one was not mine; it was three sizes too big. Too late now; the service was starting. No time to go back home and get more clothes. I just belted my pants really tightly. I dreaded putting on the coat. Yup, it was way too long; it swallowed me whole. *Just grin and go, and hope they stay up.* I needed suspenders just to hold them suckers up. I had to be *really* careful so as not to drop them on the floor. Can't you just see that picture? As I was preaching and trying to forget about it, trying really hard to preach, and praying they wouldn't fall, I overheard a couple of ladies make the comment, "Poor thing, just look how much weight he's lost."

Okay, so we made it till the next night of the crusade. I'd made the mistake of telling Steve about the suit swap. He thought that was just hilarious. He told the congregation in grand detail my predicament of the night before. Oh, what a laugh they had!

Steve and Darlene Dailey – Pastor of Mount Calvary Evangelistic Center, Indianapolis, Indiana. Photo by Barbara Pannell

But the last laugh was on Steve. It was only a couple of weeks later that sweet revenge came. They always have an annual gospel singing/cruise on the *Belle of Louisville* in Kentucky, with several groups participating. Their group planned to wear sports jackets with white mock turtleneck shirts. Steve was rushing around setting up their equipment, and at the last minute, he ran out to their motor home to get dressed. Bless his heart. You guessed it. Pulling on the shirt at the last minute, he was having a little trouble getting it on. Too tight? You might say so. Tight as a tick. Wouldn't even cover his midsection. Whoops—I think this may be Darlene's shirt. His shirt was at home. He scrambled around. Steve, son, is that egg on your face? He found a white T-shirt that would have to do. Maybe nobody noticed, except Uncle Howard. They tell me that what goes around comes around. Oh, well.

Second Trip to Heaven

A few years after the motorcycle accident, I found myself going through yet another difficult personal struggle.

God never told us that life as a Christian would be easy. He did say, though, that He would always be there with us.

This event occurred several months after my dad had gone on to be with the Lord. It had been a long day, and I was unusually tired. We had gone to bed around the usual time and soon drifted off to sleep. Sometime later, I suddenly felt my spirit leave my body. I looked down and could see my body still lying in the bed beside my wife. What a strange feeling that was!

Immediately, my spirit went through a cloud and once again into brightness. I found myself standing in the same spot that I had previously been when I'd had the accident. I saw many of the same people that I'd seen on the first trip to heaven. Only this time, I felt a big, comforting arm around my shoulder, and I heard a voice speak to me. The voice was firm, yet reassuring, strong, yet loving. It was coming from behind me. The voice said, *"Do you know that man standing over there?"*

The excitement was almost more than I could stand, as I was so astonished and excited. "Yes, that's my dad!"

"Would you like to talk to him?" I heard the voice say.

One moment my dad had been standing far off. Then it seemed instantly that he was standing directly in front of me. It seems that time has absolutely no meaning there.

It was *so wonderful* to see my dad once again. This time he looked very healthy, strong, and vibrant, such a vast difference from the nearly ninety-six-year-old blind man that I remembered him to be.

"Dad, this is the *most* beautiful place I've ever seen!" I said.

He looked at me with those beautiful smiling eyes of his and said, "Son, there's so much more to see. I wish that I could take you on inside to see it. How have you been doing?"

"I'm fine," I replied.

Dad must have known that I wasn't so "fine," as he offered this advice: "Son, don't ever look back at what you think you're missing. There's nothing on Earth worth missing heaven for." God knew that was exactly the encouragement I desperately needed to hear at this given moment in time.

Immediately, I was back in my body, quite awake at this point. My wife never stirred from her slumber. Only later, when I told her about my second trip to heaven, did she realize what a miraculous experience I'd had during that night. What a night!

Did We Miss It?

We have all seen the dazzling sparkle of an early morning frost as far as the eye can see, glittering like millions of diamonds spread out before us, like a fine carpet. Many times this awesome display of God's handiwork totally goes unnoticed as we gripe and grumble. Instead, the ice we scrape off our windshields gets our full attention.

In the rush of life, do we miss the wonder of this and other beautiful gifts? In our haste to get to our jobs, many of God's glorious creations go unnoticed. Do we also miss the fact that many of us have jobs to go to?

Have we thought about the many people who would love to have just their eyesight, that they might enjoy a beautiful sunrise or sunset? What about those who would love to have good health, so they might enjoy the great outdoors, or so they could hear the wind whispering through the pines? Do we miss the rainbows for grumbling about the rain?

Have we missed the spectacular show of the fall foliage by dreading the coming winter? Do we trade the majesty of a new snowfall because we dread cabin fever? Has the beautiful display of spring flowers been diminished by just not wanting to mow the yard?

Had we missed the awesome wonder of the birth of a new baby, how sad it would have been! I just want to remind you to take *nothing* for granted. Even the simple pleasure of watching a butterfly through the eyes of a child is a magnificent event not to be missed.

The songs of the sparrows are many times also overlooked, because of the annoying cleanup that follows their nest-building.

There's a promise that comes to mind, which God spoke to a friend during a very difficult time in her life. Many years ago, God told her, "Just as my eye is on the sparrow, so shall I watch over you." Every time she sees a sparrow, it reminds her of that precious promise that God gave her.

While at work one spring day, my friend was watching the sparrows chirping away outside the store's window as they were building their nests. They kept leaving an absolute mess with their continual flying back and forth with twigs, twine, leaves, and their droppings. My friend returned repeatedly with her broom to sweep the mess from the sidewalk, sort of grumbling under her breath about the mess they were making.

God interrupted her day by saying, *"Yes, and I love you too, even when you make a mess of things."*

Oops, no more grumbling as she continued to sweep. She knew all too well she was guilty of making a mess out of so many situations.

She still loves the sparrows and now thinks that if God can love her with all the messes she makes, she could surely sweep up after a few happy sparrows.

Greener Grass

Having been a farm boy for many years, I have watched Jersey cows pushing their heads through those old, rusty barbed-wire fences time after time. For some reason, the grass always seems greener on the other side.

Aren't we just like that! Seldom happy where we are, always jockeying for a better spot. Just trying to position ourselves in a better place is a nice way of telling God, "I don't like it here. Life ain't fair. I didn't get a fair shake. I want *MY WAY!*"

You know, the list goes on and on. Not many people actually have the audacity to blatantly shake their fists at God, but we're much more subtle in our approach.

Do, Re, Mi, Fa, So, La, Ti, Do
(Me! Me! Me!)

Sometimes we can't get past the Me, Me, Me. We get stuck there.

We've all seen the shelves full of those many coffee mugs, plaques, T-shirts, etc. that say "The King Lives Here," "King of Whatever," "The King," "The Queen," "The Queen Has to Be Obeyed," or "It's All About Me."

They're meant to be cute and funny, I'm sure. Maybe it's a joke, but it is just another way of pointing out that we have "The World Revolves Around Me" syndrome.

Are we so self-centered that we think it *really* is all about us? Have we bought into the world's standards? Are we so spoiled that we gripe about the dirty dishes or that we *have* to unload the dishwasher?

I say, "Thank God for food to eat and dishes to wash!"

Do we have a prayer list or have we resorted to a "gimme list"? Gimme this or gimme that.

Are we so transfixed on ourselves that we try to reduce God to a Santa Claus? What is this magnificent obsession with self? Is this what God wants from us? I think not. God will share His glory with no one.

And no, God doesn't have a problem with our having "things" or being prosperous. He very much desires that for us.

"Beloved, I wish above all things that thou mayest prosper and be in health, even as they soul prospereth." (III John 2)

We just have to keep the "things" in perspective.

"But seek ye first the kingdom of God, and his righteousness; and all these things shall be added unto you." (Matthew 6:33)

Do we put on our "church face" just long enough to get back in the car after services, then all hell breaks loose? Or are we "for real"?

People are hungry for God. They're searching for the "real deal." There are so many hurting people who desperately need God. There are many people searching for help and hope in a scary world. They're looking for somebody to lead them out of the darkness, somebody they can relate to. Somebody *real*.

How can we offer hope to this hurting world when we ourselves attend the First Church of the What-ifs, or are in good standing with the Whiners' Club?

There is a saying we've had hanging in our business for years: "Jesus can turn water into wine, but He can't turn whining into anything" (Author unknown).

Wash Day

As a small boy, I recall washday and that old clothesline behind the house. Who can forget the bed sheets flapping in the wind and how great those fresh, crisp sheets felt on the bed.

Nowadays, some people even complain that the clothes dryer takes too long!

Have you seen all those bottles of air fresheners, dryer sheets, and room deodorizers that guarantee "that outdoor fresh scent" all day long? Then we wonder why we sneeze, wheeze and can't breathe!

We weren't created for artificial anything. God doesn't want us to be artificial either. We can't microwave God; nor can we get an instant relationship with Him. It takes time to develop a relationship. It takes time for the real deal, time spent in prayer, reading God's Holy Word, meditating, and just being in His presence. He wants time alone with us. Quiet time spent outside in nature—just you and God—does wonders for a weary spirit. We're His children. He loves us. He wants our time, time alone with just us.

Have we missed God somewhere?

A Deer Story/However Fishy It May Sound

Deer season is highly anticipated with the Dailey men. My sons, Bruce and Lonnie, both have a love for of hunting. We enjoy the hunt itself and the wonderful meals that are prepared with our conquests, not to mention the trophies that we have mounted on the walls as reminders of our trips. My son Lonnie is the pro at hunting, fishing, and anything outdoors. He's "the man."

This was the first day of muzzle-loading season. Lonnie and I went alone on this trip. We had been out hunting early with no luck at all. Not to let it get the best of us, we thought we'd go out once more later in the day. Maybe this time we would get "the big one."

Cold as all get-out, we pulled on our camouflage jumpsuits and hunting vests before we left the house, and off we went. Arriving at the designated site, we parked the Bronco. It was starting to sleet, spitting snow, and the cold wind was stinging our faces. Now pulling on our toboggans and gloves, we were excited. Only the most dedicated hunters would go out in weather like this!

Lonnie has always been all boy from day one. He has always loved the outdoors. Not only could he survive in the deep woods, he could actually thrive outdoors. So it's always fun to go hunting with him. You know, it's always good to have a little father-son time anyway.

Having found a good spot, I sat down on the cold ground and hunkered close to an old oak tree. Lonnie went bouncing off in another direction. It wasn't long before I heard that much-anticipated crackle of leaves. My heart beat faster, as I tried to be as still as possible and remain unnoticed. I ever so slowly moved my gun into position. The big buck was now in perfect sight. I pulled the trigger. At the exact same time, a doe ran right up beside the buck. Would you believe, the bullet went through *both* deer! What a stroke of luck. Do I have bragging rights or what?

Lonnie heard the shot and rushed over to see that one of the deer was dead and the other one was still flopping around. In one swift move, he jumped on top of it and slit the deer's throat. Proud of our conquest, we each dragged one out of the woods and loaded them in the back of the Bronco, which was already full of stuff, so we barely had room enough to put them. We laid them on their backs with their feet sticking straight up in the air.

We then drove about a mile to a wide creek. We backed up close to the water so we could field dress them. When we opened the back gate, the buck fell out feet first, and "surprise, surprise" as Gomer Pyle used to say, that booger took off running!

I yelled for Lonnie to run and catch that deer. It ran across the creek with Lonnie right behind it. Neither one could run as fast as he normally could. The deer was already wounded, and the sleet, snow, wind, and leaves were making things very slick by this time. Lonnie then stopped to catch his breath. The deer stopped to catch his breath. Lonnie chased it again. It ran again. Panting and out of breath, they both stopped. Then up the mountain it ran again. I once again yelled at Lonnie, "Don't let it get away!" Not after all of this. I made my way about a hundred yards up the mountain and found a little ledge to perch on. Somehow, Lonnie lost track of the deer and yelled back at me that he thought it must have come back down past me. At that moment, I spotted it running back down toward the creek, and I got another shot off but missed this time. I was squatting down, frantically trying to reload my gun. Glancing up, I spotted the deer down by the road. Suddenly I lost my footing, just as I was trying to get another shot off. My feet went flying out from under me. I held my gun over my head with both hands in an effort to save the gun at all costs. I slid all the way to the bottom of that mountain and landed in the ditch with the deer. I got up and shot it once again. I jumped on it, "He-Man" style, and held it down until Lonnie got there and slit its throat a second time. This deer was either really tough or it was a comedy of errors. What a day!

Howard and the "big buck"

"As the hart [deer] panteth after the water brooks, so panteth my soul after thee, O God. (Psalm 42:1)

With all the extreme physical exertion and excitement of the day, one would never know that I had lain paralyzed a few short years earlier. Only God could turn a person's life around so dramatically! There's always hope when God has a calling on a person's life. Life is very fragile, and sometimes we forget just how very fragile it really is.

"Whereas ye know not what shall be on the morrow. For what is your life? It is even a vapor, that appeareth for a little time, and then vanisheth away." (James 4:14)

Here today, gone tomorrow. Are you ready for tomorrow? Are you ready for eternity?

"Train up a child in the way he should go, and when he is old he will not depart from it." (Proverbs 22:6)

"All thy children shall be taught of the Lord; and great shall be the peace of thy children." (Isaiah 54:13)

"...A wise son maketh a glad father..." (Proverbs 10:1)

Reflections Through Bruce's Eyes
(Bruce's recollection of his father's accident)

My dad was the best father any kid could wish for. Growing up, we knew that he loved us and thought we were very special. When Dad came home from work, the household was a flurry of activity. He was a cut-up and a fun dad. He always provided very well for us, and life was good.

I was in the hay field with some men hauling hay when Uncle Herman came out there and told us that Dad had been killed in a motorcycle accident. It was not that I denied that fact, but I knew he would live. Everybody was telling me that he had been dead and had come back to life, but they did not expect him to live. I just knew differently. God gave me a peace about it.

We rushed to the small county hospital in Livingston, Tennessee, where they had taken my dad. I was allowed to go into the emergency room where they were working on him and be with him for a few moments. I saw those stainless steel drainage tubes draining blood from his chest. He was on a respirator. There were all kinds of tubes and monitors hooked to him. This was a gruesome sight for anybody to see, much less a kid.

During this time we had a "conversation" of sorts. It's hard to explain, but words were not used. Nor were they formed, except that Dad knew my thoughts as I knew his answer before the thoughts were even fully formed in my mind. Although words were never uttered, we each knew exactly what the other one had said.

I heard Dad say, "Everything's going to be fine."

I "asked" him if he was in a lot of pain, and he said no.

I thought, "Dad, if I could just take your pain for you, I would."

"No, I wouldn't let you do that," was Dad's reply. "Tell Mom to not rush to get here and get hurt herself. Tell her to take her time." He said to tell her that he was okay.

With a baseball-sized lump in my throat and a respirator in Dad's, there was just no way audible words could have been spoken.

But God let us understand each other.

Life after this accident changed dramatically. The comfortable, stable, fun-filled life had now shifted. Many unsettling days, nights, weeks, months, and years lay ahead. Even as children, we knew for years that Dad's life and our very existence were in the balance.

I had not thought of this in such a long time—the whole ordeal was such an emotional period in my life, one tends to push it far away. Sometimes one forgets just what miracles really did take place, and how God's hand of mercy kept us. Sometimes one forgets how God calls us personally to be his witnesses. We are the only Bible some people ever read. We must ask ourselves, just what did they read this day?

Before the accident, we had been a busy family. Dad was always helping somebody in need, going anytime, day or night, to pray and help people. Dad was constantly preaching and pastoring churches. We cut our teeth on church pews. Now, abruptly, all this changed. We were the ones on the other side, now needing help in every way. It was a hard position to be in. It was hard on the whole family.

Eventually, at age sixteen, I quit school and went to work at a nursing home to help pay the bills. I never minded working. We all did what we had to do to help out.

Watching my dad being the example of a man of God, and growing up in church, being in those very anointed services, I also felt the call of God upon my life at a very young age. One never forgets times such as these. Though sometimes we tend to push our memories way to the back, I've learned just from watching my dad's life that God has a way of making us very miserable until we re-awaken to the call He has placed on our lives.

A young man, at a tender age, also said "Yes, Lord, I'll serve you."

"My son, hear the instruction of thy father, and forsake not the law of thy mother." (Proverbs 1:8)

Tina's Story of her Father's Accident
(written by Tina Ayers)

I'm not sure what to write, but Dad asked me to write about his accident. You know, I've spoken about it to others for years, but to sit and think back to that moment is like reliving the pain and sadness we felt that day.

You have to know I've been especially close to my dad. He has always been energetic, a hard worker, and strong. In my eyes, he was close to perfect. He was a good dad, but he did make us mind. He worked at a machine shop by day and as an auto mechanic in our garage when he came home at night. He was a deacon at our church. He headed up a church softball team and still had time for us. His extended family was mostly in Tennessee, and it was his dream for us to come back here to live. I didn't know how serious he was until he told us we were moving to Tennessee so that he could open up a gas (service) station. I am not sure I was very thrilled about it, but Bruce and Lonnie were ecstatic. They loved the country, where they could fish and hunt. I loved to fish and be outdoors too, but I didn't want to leave the city or my Grandpa and Grandma Coffman. But we did.

In Tennessee, we had a beautiful house built in a community called Walnut Grove. It reminded me of *Little House on the Prairie,* and my dad had his dream job, a service station of his very own. He could work on cars and be around old friends and family. He was pretty happy. Business was very good, and everyone loved my dad. He never met a stranger.

Life was different and difficult for me in Tennessee, even though I was young. It felt like a step back in time. I was just thirteen, almost fourteen, and totally miserable. I was used to riding my bike down paved streets for miles on end every day running to the store up the street and even getting a Big Mac just a couple of blocks down from our house. In Tennessee, our new home was the same as hell on earth to me. There was no cable TV, nowhere to ride my bicycle, and no stores for miles. Everyone knew everyone's business. This was something that was unfamiliar to me. My brothers were younger, so I don't think they had any complaints about the wide-open spaces that we now lived in. I remember complaining more than I should have about what Dad had done to us. My mom would always tell me to just give it time, but that was something I really didn't want to do.

I didn't see my dad much once we moved here, because his time was consumed by this new business venture. I missed him. About the only way I could spend time with him was to catch a ride with anyone going to his workplace or call in sick from school during the day so I would have to stay with him there, at work. However, he didn't want me hanging out there because of all the men who were around, so he would find a way to get me back home. It hurt my feelings, because I did not think he wanted me to be around him. Of course, I know better now, but at the time, I just felt abandoned.

After some time, my mom, Lonnie, and I made a trip back to Michigan to visit my mom's parents. Dad couldn't go because of his work. It felt very good to go back to what I knew as home. I was able to go to my old school for a visit, to see old friends, and love on my Grandma and Grandpa. I didn't feel bad having to leave my dad there, since he was so headstrong about making this work out in Tennessee and making it our home from now on. I was getting a little more used to it, but my dad and I had lost a bond we once had. I don't think he ever knew it, because he worked so hard, but I did.

I remember the day my aunt Annette, my brother Lonnie, and I went to some kind of a carnival. We had so much fun. It was a happy day until we got back to my grandpa's house. When we walked in the door, I could tell something was wrong. Everyone was sad. My mom took Lonnie and me into the back hallway, by my grandparents' bedroom, and told us that there had been an accident. My dad was hurt very badly. I remember falling to my knees and sobbing. I finally asked if he was dead and she said no, but she didn't know if he was going to make it. My brother and mom were crying, although she was trying to be strong. She got us together and made a plan to get us "home" to my dad in Tennessee.

I felt so much guilt, like it was my fault this had happened. I had been so upset with him for making us move there. I was selfishly thinking he had ruined my life, and now he was struggling just to stay alive. I wanted to tell him how sorry I was, that I wasn't mad at him, and that if he would hold on and get better, I would never complain about anything again. I prayed that he would hold on, because I wanted and needed my daddy back.

We flew to Nashville; it seemed like it took forever to get there. When we arrived at Baptist Hospital, we got on an elevator to go to the critical care unit. The elevator door opened, and we stepped out into the waiting room. I couldn't believe how many people were in the waiting room. I didn't know who all these people were, and someone said that they were all there for my daddy and for us. They were on their knees, praying out loud for God to touch my dad, to spare his life, and to heal him. I don't know why I was so surprised, but I was. I didn't want to talk with any of them, though. I didn't want anyone to say that my dad might not make it or that he was dying.

The doctor talked with my mom and then let us go back to see him. He told us that Dad probably wouldn't make it. I couldn't believe that. My dad and mom believed that God could do anything, so why wouldn't He help him now, just when Dad needed him the most?

I wouldn't have known it was my dad if they hadn't told us. He had tubes and wires protruding out all over his body. I didn't want to cry in front of him, but I couldn't control my tears. I wanted him to live. I wanted to tell him I was sorry and that I would live anywhere and that I'd be happy. I remember holding his hand and looking into his eyes, and I never had to speak a word. He knew. My brother Bruce became the man of the family at that moment. He was tender but stern when he spoke to my dad. I don't know exactly what he said to him, but it was enough for my dad to pull strength from him. It gave him faith.

The doctors said that he probably would not live through the night, but he did. The next day, the doctor said that *if* Dad lived, he would probably be paralyzed. Soon after that, Dad wiggled his toes! The doctor told us, "The man upstairs must be in control of him, because this was coming from a higher power," and we should keep on praying.

I knew my dad was strong, and with his faith and all of ours, God was going to pull him through, and He did. It took a long time—years—for him to recover, but he recovered, with God's help.

I believe that God had another plan for him, and this was the path that we all needed to travel to get there. If anyone ever says, "I don't know if I can do it" when they are in a valley, I tell them about my dad and our family, so that will help build their faith in God.

I'm so thankful for my dad and my mom's faith in God and their strength as a family. If we hadn't had that, we would not be where we are today, alive and a witness for God.

"And thou shalt love the Lord thy God with all thy heart, and with all thy soul, and with all thy might.

And these words, which I command thee this day, shall be in thine heart:

And thou shalt teach them diligently unto thy children, and shalt talk to them when thou sittest in thine house, and when thou walkest by the way, and when thou liest down, and when thou risest up." (Deuteronomy 6:5–7)

Lonnie Remembers
(taken from a letter written to the author, by Lonnie)

It was a beautiful June day in 1977. I was twelve years old and just full of myself! Going to Michigan with my family was an exciting event, to see my grandparents and to revisit the places where I had grown up.

This particular day, my aunt Annette had treated my older sister Tina and I to a carnival that was set up in a mall parking lot. We were all having a great time. My, how hungry a growing boy gets with all the wonderful aroma of popcorn, hot dogs, and cotton candy floating through the air! My aunt Annette bought us all we could hold, and we were having a blast riding all those fun rides!

Suddenly the strangest feeling hit me. It was an overwhelmingly sick feeling in the pit of my stomach, and I knew something was terribly wrong. Fear gripped my spirit, a feeling of sheer terror increasing with each passing moment. I knew something very bad had happened to my dad. Maybe he was even dead. A feeling of doom came over me, so strong that I felt like throwing up. I started crying uncontrollably. Tina and my aunt thought I must have eaten too much, and with all of the excitement, I had just made myself sick. I finally gained enough control of my emotions that I could at least tell them we had to immediately go back to my grandparents' home because I felt that something very bad had happened to Dad. We weren't very far from their house, but it felt like it took forever to get there.

When we got to their house and out of the car, Tina and my aunt hurried to the front door. Just as they opened it, I fell to my knees, sobbing. I knew instantly that whatever I was going to hear on the other side of that door was going to change all our lives forever. Through the tears that just couldn't be stopped, I slowly raised my head just barely enough to see through the open door. Tina and my aunt then helped me get up and inside. The sight of my grandparents standing around Mom, everybody crying but trying their best to comfort each other is a sight I'll never forget. The anguish in my soul was overwhelming, almost more than I could bear.

They told me that Dad had indeed been in a terrible motorcycle accident and that he wasn't expected to live. We all knelt and prayed for God's mercy and to spare Dad's life.

We had driven to Michigan, but since we had to get back as soon as possible, Grandpa took us to the airport. Upon arriving in Nashville, some family members picked us up and drove us to the hospital. Uncle Dickey met us at the door and told us that Dad was in very bad shape and was not expected to live through the night. He told us how Dad's liver had exploded like a watermelon that had been dropped on the floor, his ribs were broken, his back was broken, and he was on life support.

It's not that we denied what we were told, but we were praying in faith that God would heal him! We kept on praying, and he made it through the night! I jumped up and down, praising God. The doctors said they'd never seen anybody's liver go back together and start functioning as his had done. They then said that he was paralyzed and would never walk again. But after years of torment, trauma, and the grueling recovery process, he was able to walk again—ever so slowly at first, but he was walking. My dad is a very determined man, and my God is a very faithful God. The day he started walking I was so happy!

I thank God over and over for His mercy that has kept us all these years, for giving Mom and Dad the strength and faith that they needed during this incredible journey.

My parents have always been there for me, through thick or thin, no matter whether I deserved it or not. Isn't that just like our God! He loved us before the foundation of the world. He chose us. He chose me. My parents have always been like a light shining in the darkness. They've been a wonderful Christian example to me, one that exemplifies God's great love toward us. I pray that I can also be that kind of witness to others wherever I am, that I can be that light on a hill and not hide it under a bushel basket. I pray that whatever I'm doing, others will see Christ in me also. Thank you, Mom and Dad, from the bottom of my heart, and more importantly, I thank God for loving me and for His underserved mercy towards me.

Mom and Dad, consider this the biggest hug I could possibly give you! I love you and I thank God each and every day for you.

"Father God, I come to You in the name of Jesus. I want to thank You, Lord, for my mom and dad, and for all the blessings that You have poured out on them. Please, Lord, keep Your protective hedge around them and keep them safe from all evil. I praise You and thank You, Father. Amen."

I love you, Mom and Dad. God bless you.

—Lonnie

Children of Howard and Thelma: Bruce, Tina, and Lonnie. Photo by Barbara Pannell

Let Us Not Be Ignorant
Howard's Message to the reader:

Tragically, for far too many years, I had attributed the unsettling and disturbing dreams that I had just before the motorcycle accident as being "visions" from God. I had allowed myself to continue to be deceived. Nowhere in my denominational background had I been taught the insidious deadly trap that is often set for us. Many times, Satan portrays himself as an angel of light. One of the many tricks he uses is to mix just enough truth with his hideous lies to suck us into a horrible disaster! He does not play fair. He came to kill, steal, and destroy. The more of a threat we are to Satan, the harder he will throw his arsenal at us. We must be on guard at every moment. Christians are a marked people, and Satan hates us.

It was years before I realized that the dreams I'd had those three nights of the revival were from Satan and *not* from God. They were mixed with just enough truth to cause me to be more vulnerable and believe the dream about my own death was from God. It never occurred to me that they were from Satan. My agreeing with this demonic prophecy actually *caused* the wreck. Now let me repeat what I just said. My *believing* these nightmares, which I had previously thought were "visions" from God, actually *caused* the demonic prophecy to take place! Despite my own vulnerability and ignorance, God in His sovereignty mercifully intervened and said, *"I'm performing a miracle. I'm letting you live."*

We have no excuse for ignorance, since we have the written Word of God. We must take responsibility and *read* it for ourselves. We must seek the face of God and continually pray for wisdom and revelation knowledge and understanding. We must seek the discernment of spirits, whether they are from God or Satan. For every good gift that God gives us, Satan has a counterfeit that he uses for our deception and ultimately our destruction.

Dreams, visions, and premonitions that are disturbing are *not* from God and should be immediately rebuked and cast down. Cancel the assignment that Satan has on the person, whether it is for someone else or for you. Plead the blood of Jesus over the situation, as there is power in the blood of Jesus. There is wonder-working power in that all-powerful name. There is power in the *spoken* Word of God. What Satan intends for our harm, God can turn around and use for His glory! But, oh what lives are ruined and time wasted because of our lack of knowledge.

"My people are destroyed for lack of knowledge..." (Hosea 4:6)

One day, while I was working in my car-care center, someone gave me a nice denim jacket. Paying absolutely no attention to the design on the back, I put it on and wore it. I needed a work jacket, and it was comfortable. Years later, as I learned more about how easily we can be deceived, I realized that those were satanic emblems and words printed on the back of that jacket, which immediately attached a curse to me the moment I slipped it on. Unknowingly, at that moment, my life was in danger, marked with a bull's-eye right on my back, innocently going about my everyday business. I've learned we must continuously guard our minds, hearts, and lives against all evil; filter all that comes to us by the Word of God. Evil can attach itself to us by places we go, people we associate with, items we wear, posters, music, TV, and computers, just to name a few.

No doubt I had run from the call that God placed on me to preach His Word. No doubt God kept us, protected, and provided for us. In God's wonderful mercy I am able to once again preach and work with joy and a very grateful heart. I give God all the glory!

Remember that just because one may be "born again," that certainly does not make us immune to Satan's attacks. In fact, we are much more of a threat to him, so therefore, we are attacked more often. If not us directly, then he will go after whatever is most precious to us.

There are some people who would argue with you that Christians cannot be possessed with demons. I won't argue that case. Whether possessed or oppressed, if Satan is in you or on your shoulder, he is bothering you, and the power that he has over you *must* be broken, disconnected, immediately gotten rid of! It's urgent to find someone who has experience in the deliverance ministry to assist you.

We have a wonderful promise that we can depend on!

"...Because greater is he that is in you, than he that is in the world." (1 John 4:4)

We must learn the Word of God, memorize it. Get it in our spirits. Speak the Word of God out loud. Ask God for wisdom. He says he will give wisdom liberally to *all* who ask. We must learn to pray the Word of God. There's wonder-working power in the blood of Jesus!

We should never be satisfied with "tradition," just because it was what we were taught. We have no excuse for ignorance of God's Word. Read it for yourself. Don't just take somebody else's word for it. They could be dead wrong!

If you find yourself in need of deliverance, please find someone who is experienced in deliverance. This is not intended to be a manual on deliverance, but the story of my life. There are many wonderful books written on the subject, and ministers and lay people who can help.

Give It Up

God has placed a very powerful anointing on my life. Even as a child, I realized there was something very different about my life. I did not realize exactly what or why, but I knew that when I prayed, God answered. I finally gave all of myself to God's call on my life.

I had previously been torn between the calling that God had placed on my life of preaching His Word, raising my family, and having a business. Little did I realize God didn't even want me to choose between one or the other, but to put God first, and I could still have a family and a business. Once one gives up the struggle with oneself to let go and let God have His way, one can be at peace, both with himself and the world.

God puts some wonderful desires in our hearts. Nobody on this earth is perfect. I'm definitely not perfect. Only Jesus Christ was perfect. God just wants our obedience.

The anointing has always been so powerful, even in my early ministry, it often takes me by surprise. I always feel inadequate to preach the gospel, but God uses me in spite of myself.

If we ever get to where we think we're qualified, then God can't use us.

Dr. Steve Dailey once said, "Your greatest usefulness will happen when you totally depend on God and realize we have absolutely nothing to do with it."

The messages that God gave me, even in those early services, were very powerful. People came for miles to hear the little country preacher from Tennessee. Churches were packed out, with standing room only, even standing outside the doors trying to hear. I'd work all day and preach at night. Many times, revival broke out for weeks on end. Brush arbors were held for weeks at a time. Many miracles, deliverances, and supernatural manifestations have been and still are being are experienced. I've seen many people saved and lives transformed. I've seen the dead raised on several occasions and expect to see many more!

This book is not about perfection. I'm human and have many flaws and problems. Within these chapters, I hope that you see that I've not tried to cover the imperfections, nor am I proud of them, but it does show that God can use even our imperfections for His glory if we only let Him.

I've looked death in the face on several occasions. I realize I've used this verse in this book already, but it was so vital to my restoration, it bears repeating as many times as needed. When the doctors have said I couldn't live, I stood on this promise.

"I shall not die, but live, and declare the works of the Lord." (Psalm 118:17)

God wants to be first in your life or not at all

The accident, my resulting death, my visit to heaven and "return" to my body, and my recuperation left me with lots of time to ponder life and death. To see God's hand at work through all this gave me a fierce determination to tell as many people as possible that God sent His only begotten son Jesus Christ to die in our place. He paid our sin debt for us. I want people to know of God's great love for us. Jesus loves us, and He has prepared a place for us. God has prepared a mansion in heaven. What a deal! A free gift, but we do have to accept it for ourselves. We're not on autopilot.

Life is so very short. We have no promise of tomorrow or even the next breath. When we are children of God, children of the King, we should have no fear of tomorrow, no fear of death. One instant, we're here on Earth; the next instant, we could be in eternity.

As long as God gives me breath, I will continue to proclaim the good news of the gospel of Jesus Christ.

One Question, Please

Friend, please allow me to ask you a question: If you died today, right this second, where would you spend eternity? Would it be heaven or hell?

When we die, we don't just cease to exist. We will either be in heaven or hell. But you may be saying *a good God wouldn't send us to hell.* You're right. Being a good God, He made a way of escape.

God sent His only Son, Jesus. He came into this world as a baby; lived a perfect life. He knew no sin. He gave His life on that old rugged cross, He was buried, arose from the grave victorious the third day, and forever sits on the right hand of the Father, making intercession for us.

He died so that you and I would not have to. He has already paid your sin debts for you, so that you would not have to.

Now, friend, it's up to you. You have a choice. All you have to do to go to hell is nothing. That's right, ignore it. Hell is for eternity. That's a long, long time. Hell is forever; no escape. It is a literal burning lake of fire.

"And death and hell were cast into the lake of fire. This is the second death.

And whosoever was not found written in the book of life was cast into the lake of fire." (Revelation 20:14–15)

Heaven is a choice. It's called salvation; getting saved. It's real. It's forever. It's wonderful.

Remember, I died as a result of the motorcycle wreck. I've already been to heaven. I know how wonderful heaven really is. But God performed a miracle and sent me back to Earth. Maybe I came back just so I could reach one person and rescue them from going to hell. Maybe that one person is you or someone you love very much. It's a sobering thought. Think about it. When I die, I *know* I'll be going back to heaven. This time, it will be forever.

"For God so loved the world, that he gave his only begotten Son, that whosoever believeth in him should not perish, but have everlasting life." (John 3:16)

"For all have sinned, and come short of the glory of God." (Romans 3:23)

"For the wages of sin is death; but the gift of God is eternal life through Jesus Christ our Lord." (Romans 6:23)

"That if thou shalt confess with thy mouth the Lord Jesus, and shalt believe in thine heart that God hath raised him from the dead, thou shalt be saved.

For with the heart man believeth unto righteousness; and with the mouth confession is made unto salvation." (Romans 10:9–10)

"For by grace are ye saved through faith; and that not of yourselves: it is the gift of God.

Not of works, lest any man should boast." (Ephesians 2:8–9)

Getting "saved" is really quite simple. First you just need to realize that you are lost and on the road to hell. You need to confess that you have sinned and believe in your heart that Jesus Christ is the only Son of God. Believe that Jesus Christ died on that old rugged cross in *your* place. He was buried but defeated death and rose from that grave on the third day.

As you can see from the above Scripture, it doesn't even depend on how good we are. Lots of *good* people are in hell, just because they didn't believe in the Lord Jesus Christ. We can't be good enough, nor can we boast that we did anything to get salvation. It's a free gift! Confess, believe, receive (your salvation), and rejoice! It's that simple.

Let us know of your wonderful decision so that we can also rejoice with you.

My Focus

My focus is to share with as many people as I possibly can the good news of our glorious and all-powerful God. He is a triumphant, compassionate, and very loving God. He can turn our nights into days and our despair into laughter.

"A merry heart doeth good like a medicine..." (Proverbs: 17:22)

God still saves, and He still performs miracles today.

I want to help build up your faith in God. My preaching is not about how big our problems are, but how big our God is.

"Is anything too hard for our Lord?" (Genesis 18:14)

Speak your blessings into existence. Don't just wish them, don't just think them, but *speak* them into existence. That is a whole sermon in itself. Speak out loud so that your ears can hear what you say. Be consistent. Speak it often. Speak it when you first get up in the morning, just before going to sleep, and all in between—until it happens.

God still saves, heals, and delivers. He's the only way to heaven. Not just *a* way, but *the* only way. It's too late to tell me that God doesn't do miracles. I am a walking, talking miracle.

I've seen people raised from the dead and the sick made well. I've seen a way made when there seemed to be none. God is my "Way Maker." I try to keep my message simple. I preach Jesus Christ and Him crucified. A wise man once said, "Let the message of Jesus Christ be preached in such a simple way that children can easily understand it—then just maybe the adults will understand it also."

Years ago, God showed me that I would sometimes be preaching to very small groups of people, and asked me if I would go. I said, "Yes." He said other times it will be to very large groups, and asked me if I would go. I said, "Yes."

As an evangelist, the mission field that God gave me has expanded further than I'd ever dreamed. Getting the message of Jesus Christ out to people is my focus. There is no limit to what God can do.

"Now unto him that is able to do exceeding abundantly above all that we ask or think, according to the power that worketh in us." (Ephesians 3:20)

Fence-Straddling

Good news is sometimes hard to find. It is very distressing these days to even turn the TV on. Turmoil, disasters, unemployment, and unrest are on every side we turn. I do not even have to tell you we are living in very perilous times. One could easily give in to fear. But my God said:

"For God hath not given us the spirit of fear; but of power, and of love, and of a sound mind." (II Timothy 1:7)

The ups and downs of the economy could cause one to go into a tailspin, but my God says:

"And the Lord shall make thee the head, and not the tail..." (Deuteronomy 28:13)

This is a most crucial time in history. We as Christians *must* pray for our nation and for our leaders. Fence-straddling time is over. Dear people, if we ever needed to seek the face of God, it is now! As a nation, we can't wait. Now is the time.

"If my people, who are called by my name, shall humble themselves, and pray, and seek my face, and turn from their wicked ways; then I will hear from heaven, and will forgive their sin, and will heal their land." (II Chronicles 7:14)

People, did you hear that? Humble yourselves, and God will fix the mess we have gotten ourselves into. What a promise! That is the answer. We *must*, as a Christian nation, one that values our freedoms, our liberties, *humble* ourselves and *pray* before it's too late! We can't wait for somebody else to do it. *Now is the only time we have!*

Praise God in advance for the victory. Praise God relentlessly. Humble yourselves, and pray, pray, pray!

Just Call Me a Blessed Man

The alarm clock goes off way too early for me. Seems it was only moments ago that I just climbed into bed. Then I remember that I am so blessed to be able to climb out of my bed. I am delighted to have a reason to get up each morning. I am a thankful man.

As I sit on the edge of my bed, stretching a bit, I really am glad to have that alarm clock, as annoying as it can sometimes be. I recall a time I didn't have a comfy bed with warm quilts for the cold winters and cool air for the hot summers.

Wiggling my bare toes in the carpet, powerful memories come rushing in. There were those awful days after the accident, when nobody thought I'd ever be able to feel my toes, much less wiggle them.

Sometimes we need to step back, take a deep breath (and thank God we're able to take that breath), look around, and just take inventory of the many blessings we have. I am surrounded by my wonderful family and friends, for which I am truly grateful. I'm thankful for the trust that God placed in me to preach His gospel, even if He had to repeatedly tug at my heart to get my full attention. I'm so very thankful for salvation. Wow, what a blessing!

As a nice hot shower and clean clothes beckon me … wait … what is that sliding down my face? Could it be a tear? Naw, that's just liquid gratitude for all the undeserved blessings that God has given me.

Howard and Justin Looper. Photo by Barbara Pannell

Howard preaching. Photo by Barbara Pannell

Linda Easterbrook, blowing the shofar during a service. Photo by Barbara Pannell

Herman Dailey (brother), Beulah Morgan (sister), Howard and
Roy Dailey (brother). Photo by Chuck Dailey

Dr. Dean Lunsford of Logos University located in Jacksonville,
Florida, presenting Howard with doctorate of Divinity degree.
Photo by Chuck Dailey

Thelma and Howard. Photo by Barbara Pannell

Howard – Photo by Barbara Pannell

A Few Short Miles

As I sit here in my office, looking out my window, I realize I am only a few short miles from where that tiny cabin once stood—the same cabin where I made my grand entrance into this world, kicking and screaming.

Lots of days have since come and gone. I have endured many trials and struggles but never forgot the laughter and the good times. When all is said and done, there's one thing for sure that I want you to remember: God is faithful. He is always faithful.

As long as we're on this Earth, there will be trials. There's always one more mountain to climb, but the view from the mountaintop is worth the climb. In fact, the view is absolutely amazing! God will always be there, and He is always faithful.

Miracles happen when you get self out of the way, and then everybody knows that God is the one that performs them. We just have to be obedient.

Each and every day that I am blessed to be able to get up, I choose life.

"...I have set before you life and death, blessing and cursing: therefore choose life, that both thou and thy seed may live." (Deuteronomy 30:19)

At the time of the accident, God told me that He was performing a miracle and letting me live. I thought that meant that I would be totally and instantly healed, but that was not the case. Like Paul, I too have a thorn in the flesh, but God's grace is sufficient.

"...there was given to me a thorn in the flesh ...

... My grace is sufficient for thee: for my strength is made perfect in weakness.

... For when I am weak, then am I strong." (II Corinthians 12:7–10)

I still have lingering effects that I deal with on a daily basis, although most people never know, because I smile and go on. Life is still real and sometimes *very* hard.

That first gentle tug was the first of many tugs on my heart to get my full attention. Each time a deaf ear was turned, "the tug" got firmer and firmer, until one day I was jerked up short. After the accident, there was no more rope to run with, no more places to hide, but lots of time in which to ponder my life.

I often wonder about that pivotal day when the stranger walked into my business. Then, after riding my bike for a few hours and returning it, he had cautioned me about the front fork not being "quite right." Was this one last warning from God? Had I entertained an angel, perchance? Many times I've thought just how different life might have been had I pondered more on his comments, even checking the bike for some kind of mechanical failure, or skipping that fateful ride.

I do know that our actions are like a pebble that has been dropped into a quiet pool of water. It creates ripples that cannot be stopped by human hands. Once the pebble has fallen, we cannot call it back. We cannot reverse the ripples that it creates, but *know* they have far-reaching ...

The abrupt ringing of the phone jolts into my thoughts, as I instantly grab for the receiver. "Hello ... yes, this is Howard ... uh ... okay ... which hospital are they taking them to? Tell them I'm on my way."

The phone is left dangling over the side of the desk. In one quick motion, I grab my cell phone and car keys, rushing out the door as I yell back over my shoulder, "Honey, don't wait up for me."

She already knows this will probably be another long night.

About the authors:

Howard Dailey resides in Cookeville, Tennessee, with his wife Thelma, only a stone's throw from where he was born. His family includes three children, eight grandchildren, and eight great-grandchildren. Beginning his formal ministry in 1976, he has been a pastor, an evangelist, and continues to preach at countless revivals and crusades.

On October 10, 2006, he was very blessed to receive an honorary doctorate degree in Divinity from Logos University, located in Jacksonville, Florida. The certificate was presented by Dr. Dean Lunsford of Jacksonville, Florida, and Dr. Randy Moore of Lehigh Acres, Florida.

Although his ministering schedule is tight he continues to find time to operate his health food store where his expertise in reflexology and herbs are in high demand.

Photo by Chuck Dailey

Barbara Pannell and her husband Harold live in Hendersonville, Tennessee. They have two wonderful children and one very beautiful redheaded granddaughter named Kira.

Barbara has known Howard Dailey for many years. She first went to him as a client for a reflexology session, and then later had the opportunity of managing his health-food stores. Their families became close friends, often traveling and vacationing together. They feel blessed to be a small part of his ministry's support team.

While driving to work one morning, God spoke to Barbara. *"You are to write the book."* She immediately knew which book, and her reply was "God, I'll hold the pencil, You tell me what to write." She praises God for blessing her with this privilege. *A Gentle Tug* was a labor of love. It is a true story that needs to be told.

Photo by Chuck Dailey

Visit our website at **www.howarddaileyministries.com**

LaVergne, TN USA
03 April 2011
222425LV00004B/2/P

9 781449 713355